Decorating Furniture

■

Antique and Country Paint Projects

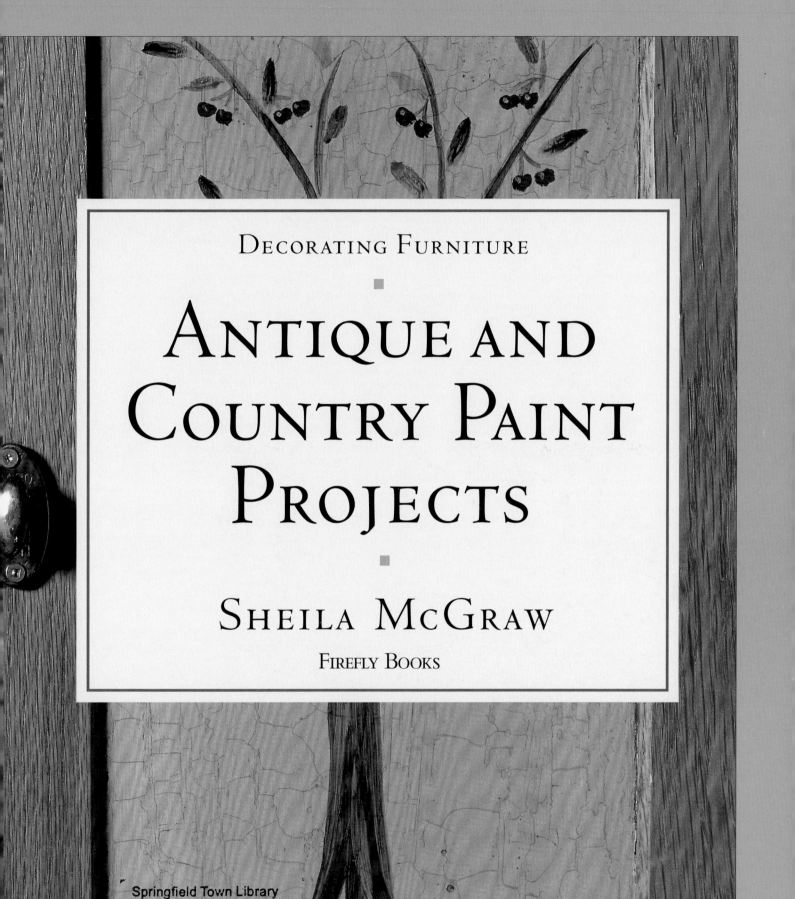

Decorating Furniture

Antique and Country Paint Projects

Sheila McGraw

Firefly Books

A FIREFLY BOOK

Published by Firefly Books Ltd. 2002
Copyright © 2002 by Sheila McGraw

National Library of Canada Cataloguing in Publication Data

McGraw, Sheila
Antique and country paint projects / Sheila McGraw.

(Decorating furniture)
ISBN 1-55297-615-7

1. Furniture painting.   2. Decoration and ornament, Rustic.
I. Title.   II. Series.

TT199.4.M327 2002   745.7'23   C2002-901443-3

Publisher Cataloging-in-Publication Data (U.S.)

McGraw, Sheila.
    Decorating furniture : antique and country paint projects
/ Sheila McGraw. – 1st ed.
[136] p. : col. photos. ; cm.   (Decorating furniture)
Summary: A step-by-step guide to furniture finishes including tools and materials, processes and projects.
ISBN 1-55297-615-7 (pbk.)
1. Furniture finishing.   2. Furniture painting.   3. Decoration and ornament.   I. Title.   II. Series.
745.7/ 23 21   CIP   TT199.4.M34 2002

Text by Sheila McGraw
Photography and cartoon illustrations by Sheila McGraw
Design by Sheila McGraw and Counterpunch/Linda Gustafson
Page production by Counterpunch

Published by
Firefly Books Ltd.
3680 Victoria Park Avenue
Willowdale, Ontario
Canada M2H 3K1

Published in the U.S. by
Firefly Books (U.S.) Inc.
P.O. Box 1338, Ellicott Station
Buffalo, New York 14205 USA

Printed and bound in Canada by Friesens
Altona, Manitoba

The Publisher acknowledges the financial support of the Government of Canada through the Book Publishing Industry Development Program for its publishing activities.

To my son Max

ACKNOWLEDGMENTS

Thank you to everyone who worked with me on this book: Lionel Koffler for making the book possible; Pamela Anthony, Melanie Siegel and Pauline McGraw-Pike for their assistance, and for lending their hands for photography. Also to Max Piersig and Jason Wing for their strong backs and sharp minds. Thank you to all who lent their furniture to this project and let me go to town on it, and to those who opened their homes to me for photography. Special thanks to The Paint Depot in Toronto for their excellent advice, their cheerful enthusiasm and their patience. Thanks to designer Linda Gustafson for gleefully knocking heads with me to get it all on paper, and to my editors, Sarah Swartz and Dan Liebman. My appreciation to all the people who work behind the scenes producing and printing this book and to the staff at Firefly Books.

CONTENTS

Introduction

■ 8 ■

Tools and Materials

■ 14 ■

Painting Basics

■ 34 ■

Projects

50

INTRODUCTION

Genuine antiques, newer furniture that has an antique finish, and furniture painted in the country genre all emanate great warmth. Well-worn patinas or folk-style paint jobs possess character and a sense of history, hearkening back to a slower-paced time. They invite touching, and they put people at ease. This is what makes rustic antiques rare — and expensive. So, incongruous as it may sound, we make our own antiques. The new techniques developed for this book allow you to antique virtually any piece: brand new, vintage or languishing somewhere in between. New products and fresh approaches allow the neophyte painter to achieve a piece that is authentically aged looking or painted with stunning country motifs. And while some treatments are more appropriate to some finishes than others, there are so many flavors from which to choose, including the romance of Victorian, the geniality of rustic, the Italianate look of stucco and the charm of English Country.

A Brush with Destiny

Many a furniture painter sets out with the simple intention of slapping a fresh coat of paint over a time-worn piece of furniture, only to have inspiration strike. The surprise result is a beautifully hand-painted work of art, a family heirloom to be cherished for generations. The flat planes of furniture — tabletops, drawer fronts and the like — present endless opportunities for decorative and pictorial techniques, while the three-dimensional form is sculptural in nature, offering many angles for viewing. Painting and decorating furniture is creativity in the round. Often the busy grain of wood, an unsuitable finish, or simply the familiarity of a piece of furniture can obscure these qualities until you stand before it, paint and brush in hand.

If you feel indecision creeping up as you try to decide on the right treatment, determine which type of decorator you are.

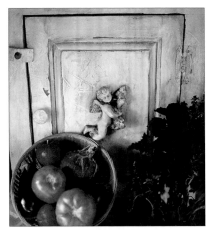

If you prefer furniture to be outstanding without standing out, think in terms of soft pastels or neutral colors and understated, tone-on-tone textures and treatments.

If you embrace the attitude that anything worth doing is worth overdoing, consider strong color, over-the-top decorative embellishments or a mixture of treatments for a grand statement.

It's no longer necessary to use slow-drying oil-based paints to achieve professional results.

Using This Book

Whether you are new to antiquing and country painting, or are highly skilled in the craft, this book will show you clearly and concisely everything you want and need to know. Beginners are shown the basics, including simple foolproof recipes for impressive treatments like crackle, distressed paint and easy freehand paint techniques, while the advanced crafter will revel in innovative application techniques. This book is more than a simple instructional guide. We have compiled a wealth of information to lead you through the maze of paints and tools available and show you how to manipulate and combine materials and techniques for wonderfully creative results. Check the *Tools and Materials* section (page 14), to acquaint yourself with the many easy-to-find and easy-to-use materials available at paint, craft and art supply stores. Unless absolutely unavoidable, only low-toxicity, water-based products are used and recommended. Water-based paints have evolved into easy-clean-up, simple-to-use, durable products.

Painting basics such as brush painting, roller painting, spray painting, staining wood and varnishing are covered, as is performing a basic paint job for those who simply wish to

> *Reading through the instructions before starting a project is like examining a road map. It helps you anticipate what's around the corner.*

paint their furniture a solid color. You'll also be referred by your project instructions to these sections as required. They provide a goldmine of basic, common-sense advice and time-saving tips.

To choose a treatment for your piece, flip through the book to find ideas that appeal to you, keeping in mind that the finished look should complement your furniture and that the projects are in a progressive order of complexity, starting with the simplest and becoming more involved as you go through the book. These advanced projects are not necessarily more difficult; they may simply require more steps, drying times or tools.

Measurements are listed in imperial units, with metric conversions following them. To make the instructions less cumbersome, the conversions are often rounded. A quart-sized can of paint is listed as a litre, for example; a yard is converted to a metre.

The projects work whether you use the imperial or the metric measurements. Finally, don't let the toy penguin who appears in the *Before* pictures throw you. This little fellow is working for scale, providing a point of reference. Without him, the size of a cabinet or some other piece of furniture could be hard to judge from the photo.

The toy penguin who appears in the Before pictures is there to provide scale, and is 9 inches (22.5 cm) tall.

Test all moving parts of the furniture.

Choosing Your Furniture

Perhaps Aunt Flossie left you a four-legged monster. It's probably a sturdy, well-built, solid piece of furniture – better quality than you can purchase today. And it's free. Instead of relegating the monster to landfill, transform it to suit your decor and get ten or possibly a hundred years of use from it. If you don't have an Aunt Flossie, garage sales and flea markets are often treasure troves of old furniture. Another possibility is unpainted furniture – especially the knockdown variety, which is ideal for painting or staining in multiple colors. And don't throw out that plastic laminate furniture. Even recently manufactured melamine-over-chipboard furniture can be transformed with specialty melamine paints.

Just as the world is divided into cat lovers and dog lovers, it is also divided into furniture painters and furniture refinishers. Refinishers feel that wood and its grain are sacred, and that every stick should be stripped and refinished. Painters, meanwhile, believe that wood is simply nature's plastic, to be transformed into painted masterpieces. The truth is somewhere in between, and this book should help balance

This new knock-down cabinet is ideal for multicolored treatments, allowing sections to be painted separately.

Original paint on an antique adds authenticity and should be left as is. Recent paint may be stripped or repainted.

Don't throw out that old kitchen or garage chair. An inspired paint job will give it new life.

the two points of view. Virtually any style, type and finish of furniture can be painted, including wood, metal, melamine and all previously painted, lacquered and varnished pieces. But please: don't paint over genuine antiques or other pieces that have historic or architectural integrity, including classics from as recently as the 1960s and 70s. If you suspect your furniture has value, have it appraised. Often, you can simply take or send a snapshot to an appraiser or an auction house. If it turns out that you own a classic, but the style is unappealing to you, sell the item rather than paint it. Antiques with original paint should be left intact. Original paint on an antique, no matter how worn, adds to its authenticity and value.

If you wish to cut down on preparation time, look for a well-proportioned piece that is solid and has a stable finish. Beware of furniture with worm holes, especially if you see sawdust on the floor around the piece – a sure sign of bugs. When they move in, these boring guests will literally eat you out of house and home. And while you can't expect perfection – the furniture is *supposed* to be old and worn – try out all moving parts to determine the aggravation factor of drawers that bind or doors that stick, especially if the vendor has them taped shut. Remove drawers to check that dovetailing is intact and that the bottoms don't sag. If chairs or tables have wobbly legs, check that they can be fixed. Bypass the item if the legs have already had surgery but are wobbling a second time.

If you are planning to apply a smooth high-gloss treatment, choose a piece with a solid, even finish in good condition. Try the

This new, poorly finished jam cupboard is a furniture painter's blank canvas, presenting endless refinishing possibilities.

fingernail test. Scratching with your fingernail should not lift the finish. Pieces with dents, scratches, cigarette burns and water or other surface damage require a busy-looking, low-luster finish to distract from the imperfections. You may wish to steer clear of pieces with water damage that has lifted veneer. Loose or raised veneer must be removed and the scars repaired, a job that requires some skill. And take a tape measure to be sure the piece fits its final destination and can be maneuvered through doors and up stairwells.

When choosing a treatment, look for finishes that will enhance the intrinsic style and accentuate the lines of the piece.

It is said that good design is form following function, and that real style is the appreciation of simple things. The art of decorating furniture captures both elusive qualities.

Choose a finish in harmony with the mood of the furniture: rustic finishes or folk painting for simple planklike constructions, decorative treatments for Victorian pieces, and English-country painting for chunky, busy pieces.

TOOLS
AND MATERIALS

This section explains the properties and functions of the tools and materials used most frequently on furniture, from basecoat through decorative finishes. Any special paints and related materials needed for a particular application are discussed in the project in which they are required; for example, information on creating "stucco" is covered in *A Florentine Finish*, beginning on page 84. If several years have gone by since your last excursion to purchase paint, you are in for a pleasant surprise. Advancements in the technology of water-based paint have led to long-wearing products with low odor, smooth texture, a huge color range, dense coverage and fast drying times. Brushes, rollers, sandpapers and many other tools and materials for applying these paints have been redesigned to keep pace. And alongside the paints and brushes, you'll find innovative supplies, kits and other materials for a huge range of treatments.

Adhesives

STICKY SITUATIONS CALL FOR GENTLE TAPES, SUPERTACKY GLUES AND DEPENDABLE PASTES

GLUE White carpenter's glue dries clear and is extremely strong. Use white carpenter's glue for bonding wood when joining or repairing pieces of wooden or painted furniture. Apply a generous amount to the join and connect the two pieces. (If repairing a piece, first clean out the join with a utility knife or sandpaper before gluing.) Wipe away excess glue and clamp the pieces tightly overnight, cushioning the clamps if necessary to prevent them from denting the furniture. If clamps aren't available, bungy cords can often be tightly wrapped around the pieces. When staining a piece of furniture, stain pieces before gluing, since the glue can act as a sealer on the wood, resisting the stain.

HOT GLUE With its fast drying time and good holding ability, a hot-glue gun is ideal for tacking decorative crafts. On furniture, it can be used for adding decorative detail or for finishing, but is not strong enough for gluing structural pieces of furniture. *When using a hot-glue gun, be careful*. This glue sticks to skin and can produce nasty burns. Some glue guns do produce a lower heat, but also a weaker tack.

MUCILAGE Mucilage is the amber-colored glue used in grade school. It comes in a slim bottle with a rubber nipple on top. Mucilage is the inexpensive magic ingredient used for creating crackled paint – the type that looks like flaking paint. The mucilage is painted onto a dry base coat of paint. While the glue is still wet, another color of paint is brushed over the glue. The different drying times of the glue and paint create the technique called crackle, which works best with latex paint. (See *Crackle*, page 54.)

TAPE Isolating areas to be painted by taping around them is called "masking." Ironically, masking tape is not a good choice of tape for this purpose. Easy-release tape, available in a light and medium tackiness, has two major benefits over masking tape. Easy-release tape is smooth and gives a crisp edge; masking tape tends to be slightly crinkly, permitting paint to ooze under its edge. Easy-release tape peels off most surfaces without disturbing the underlying finish, while masking tape often lifts paint. The only drawback of easy-release tape is its tendency to live up to its name by spontaneously falling off. The trick is to use small pieces of masking tape to tack the ends in place. Remove all tape as soon as possible after painting, preferably as soon as paint is dry to the touch. Any tape left on for long periods will leave gummy deposits or will fuse to underlying paint, tearing it off when the tape is removed.

(1) easy-release painter's tape; (2) masking tape; (3) white carpenter's glue; (4) mucilage; (5) C-clamps; (6) hot-glue gun; (7) cellulose wallpaper paste.

WALLPAPER PASTE Clear-drying, easy-to-work-with water-based wallpaper paste is the adhesive of choice for mounting large flexible materials, such as paper and fabric, to furniture. Purchase cellulose-based paste in dry form from your paint store and mix the required amount with water. This paste needs to sit for fifteen minutes or more after mixing (stir occasionally) for the granules to dissolve. Begin using the paste when it is a glutinous consistency. Use a large soft brush or a sponge to coat large pieces of paper or fabric, and use your hands to coat smaller surfaces such as découpage cut-outs and leaves. Wet pasted paper often develops wrinkles. These will shrink and disappear as the paste dries. Paper can also stretch and will then require trimming when it has dried.

SPRAY GLUE Available at hardware, paint, office supply, craft and art supply stores, this relatively new product is versatile and fast and offers a choice of temporary or permanent bond. Apply spray glue to the backs of stencils to make a light, long-lasting tack for holding the stencil in position. Spray glue can be used as a permanent adhesive for mounting fabric and posters, although it allows only one attempt at positioning. If this prospect causes anxiety, use wallpaper paste. In upholstery work, use spray glue for laminating foam to plywood, and batting to foam. Spray glue is also used for gluing block prints to a roller for continuous-printing jobs. The down side of spray glue? The overspray you get, and the amount of glue that sticks to your fingers.

When using spray glue, be careful to avoid becoming stuck on your project. This glue is tenacious. It sticks like, well, glue!

Deglossing Agents

NEW SANDPAPERS AND SANDPAPER SUBSTITUTES MAKE DEGLOSSING QUICKER AND CLEANER THAN EVER

COMPOUNDS Furniture with a lustrous finish must be deglossed before being painted, to ensure that the paint will adhere to the surface of the furniture. Very high-gloss or melamine finishes require a light sanding, but furniture that has a stable, non-flaking, low- or medium-luster finish can be deglossed with liquid deglossing agents. TSP or another liquid sandpaper can be used to dull the gloss and remove all grease and dirt. Mix the TSP with water according to the package label. Then, wearing rubber gloves, wash the piece with the solution and rinse well with clean water. Allow to dry overnight before painting.

SANDPAPER To promote the best adhesion possible between the furniture's surface and the primer or paint, lightly sand surface areas that will be getting a lot of wear, using fine sandpaper (220 grade). High-gloss or plastic laminate finishes must be lightly sanded. This is a fast job. Remember, you're only deglossing the surface, not sanding down to bare wood. Sand the surface evenly until it has a dull surface texture. When sanding raw wood, always sand *with* the grain. Sanding lightly across the grain can leave deep permanent scratches. Sanding between coats of paint with fine sandpaper (220 grade or finer) will give a smoother, lacquerlike top coat. When varnishing, sand lightly with fine sand-paper (220 grade or finer) between coats. Don't be alarmed by the cloudy effect the sanding has on the varnish. The next coat will be smooth and clear. After sanding any surface, wipe away every trace of dust with a tack cloth.

Choose the right sandpaper for the job. The grit or grade, printed on the back, indicates grains of sand to the inch. The lower the number, the coarser the texture.

EMERY CLOTH Emery cloth – black sandpaper with cloth backing, and gray-black sandpaper with green paper backing – is produced only in very fine grades. Both varieties can be used wet for sanding metal or dry for wood and metal.

GARNET PAPER Brown in color, garnet paper is the most commonly used sandpaper. Use garnet paper for sanding wood, painted surfaces or plastic laminates. Available in very coarse to very fine grades, it is ideal for virtually all sanding requirements, except for sanding metal.

(1) fine garnet paper;
(2) sandpaper for latex paint;
(3) TSP deglossing compound;
(4) coarse garnet paper;
(5) biodegradable deglossing compound; (6) emery cloth;
(7) tack cloth.

GREEN SANDPAPER Recently developed for use on latex paints and varnishes, green sandpaper won't gum up like other sandpapers do. It is available in fine to coarse grades.

TACK CLOTH A tack cloth looks like a slice of cheese in a plastic bag. Usually it comes with no instructions, one of the mystery materials sold at hardware and paint stores. Tack cloths are an absolute necessity for furniture painting and decorating. Composed of cheesecloth impregnated with a tacky substance, its purpose is to pick up all traces of dust. These cloths work so effectively, you may want them for dusting around the house.

Vacuum up any large quantities of dust. Then, remove the tack cloth from the package, but don't unfold. Instead, use the outside surfaces for wiping, until they are completely caked with dust. Then fold the tack cloth inside out and keep wiping. Continue wiping and refolding the cloth until it is completely used. Between uses, keep the cloth tightly packed in plastic so that it doesn't dry out.

You hate sanding, so why not just skip it?
No one will know. Right?

Manual and Power Tools

TOOLS PLUS COMMON-SENSE PROTECTION
EQUAL PROFESSIONAL RESULTS

MANUAL TOOLS If you are putting together a basic toolbox, the following tools are recommended. Start with a screwdriver, the type that stores several interchangeable bits in the handle. (Some of these have a ratcheting device that saves time, energy and wrist fatigue.) Next are the screws. Old furniture that has been repaired will often have mismatched screws, and no two pieces of new furniture seem to use the same type of screw. In a perfect world, there would be one type of screw, and it would be a Robertson – the square-slot type that stays on the screwdriver. A small hammer is handy for attaching wood trim and hammering in loose nails. Small- and medium-sized C-clamps, for clamping glued pieces, are a good toolbox staple. So are small and large paint scrapers for scraping loose finish, spreading adhesive and lifting stripped paint. A small, lightweight, fine-toothed hand saw is often needed for cutting various wood trims. A staple gun is also useful. Choose one that takes ⅜ in. (1 cm) staples. If you have a lot of stapling to do, consider a power stapler. (See Power Tools, below.) Acquire additional tools as you need them. Reduce frustration by storing tools in a toolbox that keeps them visible or has shallow drawers, as opposed to the type with one deep box where tools become buried and difficult to find. There's a catch, however. For the toolbox to be effective, you have to put the tools back in when you're through.

POWER TOOLS Very few power tools are required for furniture painting and refinishing. A small vibrating sander can be a handy substitute for manual sanding. Occasionally, a power drill will be required for drilling holes for hardware and leader-holes for screws. A cordless, lightweight drill with a keyless chuck is preferable. Purchase the appropriate drill bits for whatever you are drilling, wood or metal, and in the required size. A drill can also take the elbow grease out of screwing in screws. You'll need screwdriver drill bits to fit your drill. To cut plywood for tabletops or chair seats, use the appropriate saw: a table saw for straight cuts, and a jigsaw or scroll saw for curved cuts. No need to skip a project because you don't have a power saw. Many lumberyards will custom cut wood. If cutting metal, use a specialty blade. *When cutting with any type of saw, wear the necessary protective gear and watch those fingers.* If you have a big stapling job, such as a set of six chair cushions, consider springing for a power stapler.

(1) 9 oz. hammer; (2) tacking hammer; (3) hand saw; (4) screwdriver; (5) safety goggles; (6) rubber gloves; (7) jigsaw (scroll saw); (8) power drill; (9) power stapler; (10) manual stapler; (11) paint scrapers; (12) C-clamp.

Unlike hand-held staplers, most power staplers take all staple sizes. The ease of operation makes the job breathtakingly fast.

PROTECTIVE GEAR Always wear safety goggles when cutting metal, smashing tile for mosaic, or tackling any other task that can produce flying debris. When sanding, spray painting or using other materials that can produce airborne particles of paint or dust that could be inhaled, wear a paper mask that filters particles. To block both particles and fumes (or only fumes), wear a charcoal mask. For some jobs, like applying paint stripper or other toxic materials where the symbol of a hand turning into a skeleton appears on the label, gloves are an absolute necessity. Choose the heavy rubber kitchen-style gloves for these jobs. Gloves are not a necessity for most paint jobs, but many painters won't paint without them. Latex gloves – the ones that are disposable, stretchy, lightweight and thin – are perfect for painting. Wear these gloves for jobs that can irritate your hands, such as sanding, painting, rolling paint, or tiling. No more farmer's hands and wrecked manicures. If you develop a rash or hayfever-like symptoms, discontinue wearing latex gloves. You may have an allergy.

Buying tools needn't break the bank. Buy only what you need for each job, and consider renting one-job-only tools such as tile cutters or power saws.

Metallics

ANTIQUED AND PATINATED METALLICS ADD RADIANCE

METALLIC LEAF The rich patina of gold leafing is no longer the exclusive domain of the highly trained sign painter or the refinishing specialist. Imitation gold and other metallic leaf, and the necessary components of adhesive and sealer, are available at art supply and craft stores. For genuine gold, try a framing supplier. Purchase compatible products all made by the same manufacturer. Incompatible products can cause chemical reactions that ruin the finish.

Applying metallic leaf is straightforward and simple, and the results are professional looking. The adhesive is applied to the surface area and allowed to cure for several minutes. It remains extremely tacky. The metallic leaf is laid over the adhesive and burnished to make contact with it. Excess leaf is brushed away with a small paint brush. Then the leaf is protected with a coat of sealer. Leafing is available in gold, silver, pewter and copper, all of which can be antiqued or left bright. To antique the leafing, purchase antiquing paint or use watered-down artist's acrylics: burnt sienna on gold or copper, deep blue on silver. Brush on, then wipe off with a cloth.

METALLIC PAINT As an alternative to metallic leaf, paint-on metal (made from ground ore suspended in a liquid medium), available at art supply stores, provides a dense, convincing metallic finish. Don't confuse these paints with small jars of gold and silver hobby-type enamels. You'll know the right ones if they are displayed with the compatible patinas, sealer and etching fluid. Choose instant iron, gold, copper or bronze. The labels on the jars of paint include instructions for using each product. A clear sealer, which acts as a primer, is brushed on first, followed by two coats of the metal. The metallic paint can be patinated or sealed as is.

PATINA Patina is the thin sheen on a copper or other surface, produced by age. Patinating metallic paint gives an aged and refined quality to a piece of furniture.

These treatments are usually applied to molded or carved-looking decorative pieces such as pedestals; however, they are also effective on flat surfaces. Blue and green patinas are available for copper metallic paint, and rust is available for iron. Purchase the patinas wherever you buy the metallic paint. All the patinas are very watery. When brushed onto the

(1) liquid copper; (2) sheet copper; (3) patina blue; (4) primer-sealer; (5) etching fluid; (6) mica gel; (7) artist's acrylic paint; (8) liquid iron; (9) instant rust; (10) patina green; (11) copper leaf; (12) gold leaf; (13) sealer for leaf; (14) adhesive for leaf.

dry metallic paint, they begin their work, almost immediately oxidizing the metal. Apply sparingly, adding more coats to achieve the desired effect. Once the patina has finished the oxidizing process, usually three days, clear sealer is applied. Clear sealer can tone down the effect of the patina and kill the sheen of the metallic paint. It's a good idea first to do a test on cardboard to examine the effects of the sealer on the finish. If you don't seal the patinated metal, the treatment may transfer or be damaged by use.

SHEET COPPER Try hobby shops as well as art supply and craft stores for finding sheet copper. This is the copper that hobbyists use for burnishing. The sheets are as thick as heavy paper and can be cut with heavy workshop or kitchen scissors. *When cutting this copper, be extremely careful.* The edges can be very sharp. Injuries are more painful and annoying than paper cuts. (Wearing a cast-off pair of leather gloves can help protect you.) The cut edges can be sanded dull with very fine sandpaper or an emery cloth. Sheet copper can be patinated with the same blue or green patina used on metallic paints. Before patinating the copper, treat it with an etching fluid, often called metal master, which is part of the metallic paint and patina family. Then follow the same steps for patinating metallic paint.

Metallics are most effective when used as an accent rather than as an all-over treatment.

Painting Tools

INGENIOUS NEW APPLICATORS COUPLED WITH TRADITIONAL TOOLS PERMIT CREATIVE TREATMENTS

BRUSHES Purchase good quality brushes. A cheap brush will shed hair on your paint job and fuzz up like a squirrel's tail, spraying paint as you work. A quality brush will hold paint better, paint cleaner lines and endure far more use and washing, returning to its original shape and condition.

For cutting-in on furniture, choose a brush about 1½ in. (4 cm) wide. For painting large, flat sections, purchase a 2 in. (5 cm) brush. Choose brushes made for water-based paint. These synthetic brushes, unlike their natural-hair counterparts, won't get bushy from contact with water. Buy brushes with fine bristles that won't leave grooves in the paint job. A brush with a diagonal cut on the bristles makes it far easier to paint the many corners and angles of a piece of furniture.

Tackle detail work with two basic artist's brushes: a medium-sized, fine-point brush, and a square-tipped brush about ½ in. (1.25 cm) wide. These don't need to be expensive. Just be sure the fine brush will hold a point and not resemble a small palm tree. Choose brushes compatible with water-based paint products.

To prolong the life of your brushes, don't allow paint to dry in the bristles. Wash brushes thoroughly with warm water and dish soap. Rinse well and wrap each brush in a paper towel to hold bristles in shape. Lay brushes flat to dry. Standing them on their handles spreads bristles, rusts the metal and rots the handle. Standing brushes on their bristles gives them a bad perm. (For more information on painting with a brush, see *Brush Painting,* page 40.)

ROLLERS

The small, flat surfaces of furniture are perfectly suited to a small roller, eliminating brushstrokes and imparting a smooth, even texture to a paint job. Rollers are available in many sizes and materials. A small, short-pile roller is ideal. Foam rollers can hold air, creating bubbles in the paint job. (New "velvet" foam rollers have tiny hairs that pierce the air bubbles as you paint.) Bargain or high-pile roller sleeves can also make air bubbles. These can be eliminated (along with lint from the roller) by dampening the roller sleeve and rubbing it as dry as possible on a paper towel before slipping it on the handle. Choose a tray to fit the roller. A tray provides a reservoir of paint and a ramp to roll out the excess, preventing runs, sags and uneven application.

(1) synthetic sponge; (2) square-tipped artist's brush; (3) fine-point artist's brush; (4) brushes for latex paint; (5) broom for texturing paint; (6) small roller; (7) combing tool; (8) wood-graining tool; (9) natural sponge.

Roller sleeves can be washed with soap and water, but most lose their soft texture. Save them for applying primer, not the finished paint job. (For information on painting with a roller, see *Roller Painting*, page 42.)

SPONGES

Sponging paint onto a surface has become the staple texturing technique for all levels of painters. Sponges, both synthetic and natural, produced especially for use with paint, are available at paint, craft and art supply stores. Synthetic sponges are formed into a half-sphere shape and have consistent, small pores. Sea sponges have large, erratically spaced pores and are irregular in size and shape. Sponging onto furniture is unlike sponging onto a full wall. Large prints produced by a sea sponge, pleasing on a wall, look crude on a piece of furniture. The scale makes the difference. Either a synthetic or a sea sponge can be used, but try to get a sea sponge with small pores. When sponging, tear off a section about the size of a tennis ball. Holding it between your fin-

gers and making a pouncing motion, sponge sections, layering and blending colors for a suedelike effect.

TEXTURING MATERIALS

The creative painter can achieve many unique textures simply by layering paint and etching it with unexpected household items. Most texturing treatments lift a wet top coat of paint from a dry base coat with a texturing tool such as a crumpled plastic bag (smooshing), an inexpensive feather duster, or a twisted rag (ragging), or by dragging a brush through the wet paint (dragging). Shadowing is created by taping and painting stripes in two finishes – matte and glossy – in the same shade. Paint stores sell many texturing devices, including textured rollers for creating wood grain prints and combs for making even-textured stripes and basketweaves.

BLOCK PRINTS

Block printing is an effective method of creating multiple images for both the accomplished artist and the artistically challenged. You can purchase precut block prints made of foam, or you can hand cut your own prints. Purchase the thin, flexible foam used for children's cut-out crafts, or use a foam insole. After cutting out the block print, score details into the foam. These will hold more paint and print darker, giving the print added interest. Block printing can be done singly, or several identical prints can be laminated to a roller for continuous printing. Apply glazes, acrylic paint or latex paint onto the foam block (or laminated roller) and impress it onto the surface of the furniture, applying even pressure. Then lift it off. Potato printing is a form of block printing using a carved potato. Potato prints produce a naive, weathered print in keeping with many rustic and antiquing treatments. (See *Crackle*, page 54, steps 3–5.)

Paint Products

FAST-DRYING, LOW-ODOR, EASY-CLEAN-UP PAINTS, ADDITIVES AND VARNISHES ADD TO THE PLEASURE OF PAINTING

LATEX WALL PAINT Although the experts at the hardware store may insist you need oil-based paint, just keep in mind that they're probably not computer geniuses either. Times have changed. It is no longer necessary to endure the noxious fumes, glacial drying times and tedious clean-up of oil-based paints. The technology of water-based paint products means long-wearing paint in finishes from flat matte to high gloss; low odor; very fast drying and recoating times; and easy soap-and-water clean-up.

Whether you purchase a can of acrylic paint (plastic emulsion) or latex paint (synthetic rubber emulsion) at the paint store – both types are popularly referred to as latex – expect to apply two coats for solid coverage. Don't be alarmed that the paint is a light color in the can. It will dry darker. Choose a low-luster to glossy finish for furniture. Avoid flat finishes, which show fingerprints and scuff marks. Any water-based paint should be well stirred or shaken before using. Latex paint dries quickly to the touch – usually an hour – but it should be allowed to dry several hours before recoating. Consult the label for precise drying times. Water-based paints remain vulnerable and need to cure for at least thirty days before being washed or subjected to wear and tear.

ACRYLIC WALL PAINT This paint can be bought by the can at paint stores. Because it is water based, it is generally (but improperly) referred to as latex. Check the label for the actual contents. More expensive than latex paint, pure acrylic wall paint is considered the highest quality of most paint lines. But the reality is that when it dries, it has a rubbery finish that tends to stick to objects that come in contact with the surface for any length of time, lifting the paint (a problem on furniture). A better bet is a combination of acrylic and latex. You'll get the best qualities of both types of paint. Like latex paint, acrylic needs to cure for thirty days.

ARTIST'S ACRYLICS Originally intended as an alternative to artist's oils, acrylic paint has developed as a versatile medium in its own right. Available in a huge range of premixed colors and incredibly fast drying, their compatibility with latex paint makes artist's acrylics ideal for creative furniture treatments. Artist's acrylics can be used straight from the tube for an oil-paint texture or thinned with water for watercolor washes and glazes. They can also be used for stenciling, freehand painting or texturing. Generally sold in small pots and tubes, these acrylics offset the need to buy a large can of latex paint, which is too much paint for detail work.

MELAMINE PAINT The popularity of plastic laminate, particleboard furniture and countertops has helped create a generation of new high-adhesion paints, referred to as melamine paints. Unlike most other paints, which lose their grip and peel,

(1) artist's acrylics in tubes; (2) artist's acrylics in pots; (3) colored glazes; (4) latex paint; (5) glaze; (6) extender; (7) shellac; (8) spray paint; (9) primer; (10) acrylic mediums; (11) varnish; (12) gel.

these cling tenaciously to plastic surfaces. Always degloss the melamine surface by sanding with fine sandpaper (220 grade or finer) before applying the paint. Melamine paints vary from store to store. If a label indicates that a primer is necessary, use an ultra-high-adhesion, white-pigmented, shellac-based primer for best results. Allow melamine paint to cure for two to four weeks before subjecting to wear and tear or washing. If melamine paint is not available, latex paint can be substituted – so long as the melamine surface has been de-glossed by sanding and a coat of ultra-high-adhesion, white-pigmented, shellac-based primer is applied first.

SPRAY PAINT Spray paints are ideal for painting pieces of furniture with spindles or intricate molding. Spray painting imparts a dense, smooth, even coat in a range of finishes from low luster to high gloss. It also eliminates the drips, gaps and sags usually associated with brush painting.

While graffiti may have given spray painting a bad name, this art form created a demand for spray paint that has benefited the furniture refinisher with a wealth of low-odor, low-toxicity acrylic spray products in a huge range of colors. Purchase spray paint at hardware, art supply and craft stores. Also available in spray form are textured treatments such as granite and marble; paints for covering metal or rust; varnishes; and fast-drying, crystal clear lacquers. (See *Spray Painting*, page 44, for more information on the application of spray paint.) For the avid spray painter, special nozzles giving narrow to wide coverage are available at art stores that cater to the graffiti trade.

The versatile, durable quality of artist's acrylics, and their compatibility with other paints, allows creative expression on furniture.

EXTENDER Extender is added to paint to slow the drying time. Use extender when working on a painstaking technique, such as marbling, or when applying a texturing technique, such as sponging, over a large area.

Add water-based extender to latex or acrylic paint in the proportions specified on the label. Both extender and glaze can be mixed into paint at the same time. Extender is available at art supply and craft stores in smaller quantities than what you may find at paint stores.

GLAZE Glaze, a milky-looking viscous liquid, is added to paint to make the paint more transparent, while maintaining the original consistency. Add glaze for texturing and layering techniques, such as ragging, sponge painting or dragging, when you want the underlying coat to show through to a certain degree. Some painters are comfortable adding water to paint to achieve the transparency desired for sponging or similar treatments. Other texturing treatments, such as dragging, require the paint to maintain its viscosity; otherwise the paint, if too liquid, can run together and destroy the intended effect. Add water-based glaze to latex or acrylic paint in the proportions specified on the label. Both glaze and extender can be mixed into paint at the same time. Glaze is available at paint stores in larger quantities than what you may find at art supply and craft stores.

Premixed tinted glazes are available at art supply and craft stores. These are paint and glaze mixtures sold in small jars, saving you the trouble of mixing your own colored glazes. Use these glazes for small projects such as block printing, where a decorative, overlapping, sheer quality is desired.

MEDIUM AND GEL Mediums and gels are acrylic-based cousins of the glaze and extender family. They are available at

Extender and glaze are used for layered, textured paint treatments such as sponging, ragging and smooshing.

art supply and craft stores in smaller quantities than what you may find at paint stores. Mediums are milky-looking viscous liquids that dry clear and are used as varnishes. They come in a variety of finishes, from flat to glossy, and many contain ultraviolet protection to help keep underlying paint from fading or otherwise breaking down under exposure to UV rays.

Unlike water-based varnish sold at the paint store, mediums tend to have a rubbery texture when dry, which sticks to objects that come in contact with the surface. Gels are used for thickening paint or for texturing a painting surface. They are milky when dry and are available in a variety of thicknesses, from light (like glutinous soup) to very dense (like peanut butter). Some gels have additives such as paint, sand or mica to give them color and texture. Heavy gels are durable enough, when dry, to be used for a textured treatment.

PRIMER/SEALER *Primer* is more than just a first layer of paint. It adheres more tenaciously than any paint, providing a painting surface that won't peel and an even skin over the surface to prevent patchiness on uneven and absorbent surfaces. Apply primer before painting or decorating, unless you are antiquing with sandpaper (see *Cupboard Love*, page 50) or staining. Stain must be applied directly to bare wood.

Many types of primer are available. Water-based, high-adhesion primers are ideal for most furniture. Primers that are not high adhesion are good for walls, but not for furniture. If you are using a water-based primer on unpainted wooden furniture, the primer may raise the grain of the wood. If this happens, sand lightly with fine sandpaper (220 grade) when the primer is dry. Furniture with a high-gloss finish should be deglossed by washing with TSP, or by sanding before priming.

For plastic laminate finishes, degloss by sanding, then paint with a melamine paint; or use an ultra-high-adhesion, white-pigmented, shellac-based primer before painting with latex paint. These ultra-high-adhesion primers require chemical solvents for clean-up (consult the label). Or simply use a cheap disposable brush and roller sleeve. Shellac-based primer is not recommended for varnished or lacquered furniture because it can eat into the finish.

Use spray primer for furniture with spindles or intricate detail.

Sealers have two uses. First, when painting (not staining) unpainted, wooden furniture, use shellac or another sealer recommended for this purpose to seal all knots in the wood before priming or painting. Otherwise, the knot will discolor the paint. Shellac requires a chemical cleaner for brushes (consult the label). Alternatively, you could use a cheap disposable brush. Second, you'll find that clear sealers are sold with specialty treatments such as gold leaf and paint-on metallics. These are used not only as a sealer to be painted over the treatment for protection, but often also as a primer. Purchase a sealer compatible with the products being used.

VARNISH

Whatever type of varnish you use, always apply it with a paint brush. Rollers, especially foam rollers, leave bubbles in varnish.

Water-based varnishes, often called urethanes, are fast drying, with low odor and easy soap-and-water clean-up. They come in a range of finishes, from low luster to glossy, and many are non-yellowing. Varnish enriches color, somewhat like wetting down your car does, and protects your paint job against cleaners, scuffing and chipping. Several coats give a rich glasslike finish. Varnish can make the use of unorthodox materials and treatments workable, stabilizing transient color and encasing fragile materials in a durable plastic coating. It is best to varnish a full piece of furniture, though varnishing only the areas that will receive wear and tear is acceptable if a non-yellowing formula is used.

Don't view varnish as the enemy. Work quickly, avoid overbrushing and apply several coats, sanding lightly between coats. (See *Varnishing*, page 48.) Oil-based varnishes can also be used. If you find that the very quick drying time of water-based varnish makes application difficult, you may prefer oil-based urethanes. They take overnight to dry and tend to impart an amber tone to the finish. Oil-based varnish is used to create crackled varnish. (See *The Cupboard Was Bare*, page 102.)

Many a paint disaster has started on the Sale shelf — a quart of paint with a gallon's worth of tint... paint in the wrong color or finish... and paint that mysteriously never dries.

Paint Removers

NOT LIKE THE OLD DAYS – GENTLE STRIPPING AGENTS AND EFFECTIVE TOOLS MAKE PAINT REMOVAL FUN (ALMOST)

PAINT STRIPPERS If the idea of paint strippers conjures up visions of vats of steaming toxic waste, it's been a while since you tried stripping paint. There are strippers that smell like citrus fruit, and some are non-toxic enough that wearing gloves is optional. Welcome as these advancements are, stripping furniture is still a messy job, especially if the piece has intricate detail or many layers of paint and varnish. A piece of furniture with either historic or design integrity is, however, worth the journey into slime. Stripping a good basic piece buried under several coats of badly applied paint is also worthwhile, because it cannot be repainted until the

many layers are removed. But you can also partially strip such a piece, allowing sections of layered color to show through. This treatment is not only interesting and attractive, but it reveals the history of the piece.

The old way of stripping was called dip and strip. The whole piece was placed in a trough of heavy-duty toxic chemical stripper. This procedure often unglued joints and had caustic effects on the underlying wood. Most strippers today are much more gentle. Choose a gel stripper, which will cling to vertical surfaces. Placing plastic wrap over the stripper can speed the curing time. Just check first that the stripper doesn't eat the plastic. (For more information on stripping paint, see *The Cupboard Was Bare,* page 102.)

PROTECTIVE GEAR   Paint stripper will destroy the finish on your floor. Do the job over several layers of paper (newspaper is fine), with a layer of plastic or, even better (since some strippers dissolve plastic), an old bedsheet on top. Decant the stripper to paint it on. Pour it into crockery, not plastic. Wear heavy rubber gloves for this job, the kitchen type. Avoid latex surgical gloves unless you are certain the stripper won't eat through them. Safety goggles are also recommended. When you brush the stripper on and scrape off loosened paint, some particles can become airborne.

TOOLS   Using the proper tools will make the stripping go much faster and easier. In the first stages of the stripping, a medium-sized paint

(1) stripping brush; (2) rubber gloves; (3) organic stripper; (4) gel stripper; (5) safety goggles; (6) paint scrapers.

scraper is needed for lifting the bubbled, loose paint. Next, a hard plastic stripping sponge, which resembles a block of petrified spaghetti, is ideal to use along with the stripper to help lift paint. When most of the paint has been removed, use a stripping brush along with the stripping sponge. This brush resembles a barbecue-grill cleaner, with brass bristles (they won't rust) on one side and nylon bristles on the other. The nylon brush side is ideal for giving the piece a thorough rubdown. The brass bristles remove the last particles of paint and varnish from any carving and trim, and from the grain of the wood. When using scrapers and other sharp tools, remember to let the stripper do the work. Overly enthusiastic scraping can damage fine or soft wood, defeating the purpose of stripping, which is to reveal the natural, unspoiled beauty of the wood.

Hold it! Don't strip that antique! However worn and beaten-up the furniture may be, original paint on an antique adds greatly to its authenticity and value.

Specialty Products

FROM THE INSPIRED TO THE BIZARRE, NEW PRODUCTS ARE CREATED TO FULFILL THE PAINTER'S EVERY NEED

KITS A tremendous number of kits are available for techniques such as crackle, block printing, marbling, sponging and stenciling. Many of these kits are adequate for the painter, particularly if only a small area is to be painted, eliminating the need to buy large quantities of products that will go unused. However, some of the kits are pricey and don't live up to their promises, with poor instructions and materials that just don't work. Many of these techniques are actually quite simple to perform, require readily available ingredients and are demonstrated in this book.

SPECIAL APPLICATORS Manufacturers are scrambling to keep pace with the demand for innovative paint applicators. Aside from the usual brushes and rollers, there are combs (for creating striping and basketweave effects) and raised wood-grain patterns to be rolled and dragged. Most unusual are rollers that have plastic floral shapes riveted to them, reminiscent of a 1960s-era bathing cap. These rollers are used to create texture by layering similar paint colors, thinned with glaze, with the plastic attachments producing a subtle, semiregular pattern. Various sponges, rags and texturing brushes are available too, as are foam applicators for painting edges, corners and flat areas.

SPECIALTY PAINT Fashion designers like Ralph Lauren and Laura Ashley, who have become lifestyle/interior designers, have come out with signature lines of top-quality water-based paints in painter-inspiring rich colors. These paints are created to complement the housewares that the designers also produce. Although this approach to choosing a paint color may seem excessive to some, others find it reassuring and exciting, trusting that the results will be exactly as expected and that the decor and paint will be tasteful and will harmonize perfectly. Other paint manufacturers are producing innovative paints with unlimited possibilities for application. There are very thick iridescent paints, which are applied in layers with a trowel, sanded and glazed to a glasslike sheen. There are paints with tiny flecks of suspended color, which are made to be layered with similarly toned glazes to produce wonderful depth and suspended texture. There are also a variety of spray-paint effects, including a granitelike composition that comes in kit form. There is

(1) stencil cream paints; (2) stencil brush; (3) texturing brushes; (4) marbling spray; (5) flecked paint; (6) marbling kit; (7) texturing roller; (8) spray granite; (9) texturing paint; (10) synthetic sponge; (11) colored glazes.

even spray-on marble veining, although it looks rather like a mix of hair and mushy spaghetti. Instead of trying to create marble veins with it, the creative painter could have fun with the effect in other unusual ways.

STENCILING MATERIALS Purchase a precut stencil from the huge selection available, or design and cut your own. To cut your own stencils, buy stencil plastic at an art supply or craft store — the lightweight, flexible blue plastic that is semitransparent for tracing designs — and use an X-acto or a utility knife or small, pointed scissors. Lightweight cardboard can be substituted for the plastic. To execute the stencil, use any type of paint you wish: spray paint for smooth even coverage, acrylic or latex paint applied with an artist's paint brush for a freehand look with brushstrokes, or stencil cream paint applied with a stencil (stipple) brush for dense smooth coverage. The spray and acrylic paints dry quickly, while the cream paint can take as long as a week to dry. Use spray glue to provide a tacky backing on the stencil. (See *Tabletop Rose Bower,* page 66.)

Don't be intimidated by the multitude of new products at the paint store. Many can add substantially to your creative pursuits.

Painting Basics

Most projects in this book will refer you to this section to prepare, prime and paint your furniture with a base coat of paint. This base coat is the groundwork for your decorative treatment.

Step one is the preparation. Virtually every piece of furniture needs some preparation before painting or staining, whether you're repairing wobbly parts, removing doors, hinges and hardware, deglossing a shiny surface, or sanding raw wood.

Step two is applying the primer. Most furniture – varnished or painted wooden pieces, melamine pieces, or unpainted wooden furniture – requires priming before painting. Exceptions include unpainted wooden furniture that will be stained, and furniture to be painted and then antiqued by sanding. See brush, roller and spray painting information in this section to determine the method of application most suitable for your piece of furniture.

Step three is the painting. Paint is applied (usually two coats) over the primer in the same manner as the primer was applied. After the base coat of paint has been applied, the creative and inventive stage of adding decorative effects and treatments begins.

Skipping the preparation stage now may haunt you later.

Preparation

Purchase new hardware if desired. If the piece has wooden knobs, consider painting them.

In the final analysis, the preparation of the furniture – fixing loose parts and preparing the surface for painting – is more important than any painting or decorating. Avoid the temptation to skip the prep stage of painting. It will yield consequences (that mom warned you about) of the same variety as building a house on sand, eating dessert before the main course, or sleeping in an unmade bed. Different varieties of furniture will require different types of preparation. Read through this section to determine how much and which types of preparation your particular piece of furniture needs. Although many painters dread this part of the job, once it is out of the way, the paint and decorative treatments can be done with a clear conscience.

Right at the start, set up a comfortable, well-lit work area. Keep the work space as flexible as possible, with moveable light sources and a convenient table on which to work. You may wish to call off the bridge game and abscond with the card table. It's ideal for putting all but enormous items of furniture at a comfortable working height. Its small scale makes furniture accessible from all sides, and it can be folded up and tucked away when not needed. Keep a supply of dropsheets handy. Old large, non-slip bedsheets are good. Plastic or paper can be used, but don't use newspaper. The printer's ink will transfer to your paint job.

MATERIALS

The following tools and materials may be required.

- screwdriver
- machine oil
- new hardware and screws
- wood filler
- small paint scraper (or putty knife), wide paint scraper
- fine sandpaper (220 grade)
- sanding block

- wooden matchsticks
- white carpenter's glue
- clamps or a bungy cord
- power drill
- deglossing compound (TSP or other liquid sandpaper), rubber gloves
- tack cloth

1 *Drawers*

Remove drawers, marking their position (top, center, bottom, etc.) on the back panel. As a result of wear and tear or how they were built, drawers will often fit properly only in their original slots.

2 *Hardware*

Unscrew and remove all hardware. This includes removing doors by unscrewing hinges. On a dropleaf table, remove the hinges and the contraptions that keep the leaves up. Hinges should be cleaned and oiled. If a tabletop is removable, the painting will be easier if the top is removed and painted separately from the base.

3 *Filler*

If holes left by old hardware don't correspond to the new hardware, use wood filler and a small paint scraper or putty knife to fill the holes. Also fill any gouges in the surface of the piece. Sand the wood filler smooth and level with the surface, using fine sandpaper.

Fill the screw holes of loose door hinges with the wooden ends of matchsticks and carpenter's glue. Allow to dry before replacing the hinges. Hinges can also be shifted when they are replaced.

4 *Fixing loose parts*

Loose desktops and dresser tops are caused by lifting the furniture by the top instead of the base. Reattach a loose dresser top by replacing the existing screws with fatter, not longer, ones. Reglue loose joins in a chair by levering the join apart, cleaning it as much as possible, then applying carpenter's glue to the join and clamping it shut. (If you don't own clamps, you can wrap tightly with a bungy cord.) Glue and clamp loose trim. Allow all glue to dry overnight.

Loose, wobbly table legs are caused by dragging the table instead of lifting it. There are many different constructions for table legs. Try to figure out how the table and legs are constructed. Glue and clamp all joins and tighten or replace all screws.

Measure and drill holes for new hardware, if needed.

5 *Preparing the finish*

Granny furniture – old, dark wood – should be given the fingernail test. Scratch the varnish with your fingernail. It should not be marked or lifted. If it is, this loose, crumbly finish will flake when painted, taking the paint with it. Scrape off the loose varnish with a wide paint scraper – a fast job. Then sand the surface smooth with fine sandpaper, either by hand or with a sanding block.

If the furniture has a high-gloss or plastic laminate finish, it will require light sanding to allow better adhesion between the paint and the furniture surface. Sand with fine sandpaper, in the direction of the grain on bare wood (sanding across the grain can create deep scratches), and lengthwise on painted pieces.

If you really hate the dust and the effort of sanding and your furniture has a medium- to low-luster finish, clean and degloss your furniture with a deglossing compound such as TSP. Mix the granules according to instructions on the label. Wearing rubber gloves, wash down all glossy areas, rinsing well with clean water. Allow the furniture to dry overnight.

Vacuum and clean the whole piece of furniture, both inside and out. Remove all remaining dust by wiping the piece with a tack cloth. If desired, wash the piece with a damp cloth and a gentle cleaner. Allow to dry overnight.

Cats seem to gravitate to the laps of those who want them least. Naturally, they're also drawn to fresh paint. Put puss out.

Priming and Painting

Applying a coat of primer before painting is a necessary step for most projects. Exceptions include furniture to be antiqued by sanding away paint to reveal bare wood, and unpainted wooden furniture to be stained. Primer adheres more tenaciously to the furniture's surface than paint does, to provide a strong bond and an even skin. The paint can then flow onto the primer without patchiness or an uneven texture.

Primer and paint should be applied by the same method. For instance, if the furniture is simple with flat surfaces, both primer and paint should be applied with brush and roller. If the furniture has intricate carving, trim, or spindles, spray primer and spray paint should be used. Don't be discouraged by the streaky, uneven quality of primer when you put it on. Apply primer swiftly and avoid the temptation to redo areas. Primer sets and dries quickly, and reworking will tear up the surface. Once the primer is dry, the furniture can be given one or two coats of water-based paint as a base coat. If your furniture has a plastic laminate finish, use melamine paint for the base coat. (See *Melamine Paint,* page 27.) Before adding other treatments, allow the coats of paint to dry for the time specified by the manufacturer.

Touching wet paint is a universal temptation, so devise strategies to keep yourself away while items are drying. Paint just before bedtime, for example. And remember, mistakes are the mother of inventive solutions.

MATERIALS

The following tools and materials may be required.

- small quantity of white shellac
- easy-release painter's tape or masking tape
- quart (litre) high-adhesion, water-based primer; or spray primer; or, for plastic laminate surfaces, if primer is suggested on the label, white-pigmented, shellac-based primer
- painting tools:
  -paint brush, 1½ in. (4 cm) wide, for water-based paint
  -roller handle, 4 in. (10 cm) wide, and short-pile sleeves
  -roller tray to fit roller
- quart (litre) eggshell or satin finish latex paint in the color of your choice
- quart (litre) non-yellowing, water-based varnish
- paste wax, buffing cloth

1 *Choosing the primer*

If your piece has molding, spindles or carved detail, you may wish to use spray primer. (Follow the instructions for *Spray Painting*, page 44.)

2 *Priming removable pieces*

Seal any knots on raw wood with shellac before priming.

Stir primer thoroughly before applying it. Primer should be applied to all areas that will be painted.

Start with removable pieces, such as doors or drawers. Lay doors or other flat sections on supports and mask off any sections that are to remain unpainted.

If the drawers are clean, prime only the fronts and their edges. If the drawer interiors are grungy, paint them with primer.

Use the paint brush to cut-in with primer, painting all inside joins and corners that aren't accessible to a roller. (See *Brush Painting,* page 40.) Then use a roller to prime the flat areas up to the brushwork. (See *Roller Painting,* page 42.)

The exterior sides can be primed if desired, but make sure there is enough space between chest and drawer. (Adding coats of primer and paint to the sides can cause drawers to bind.) Water-based primers and paints dry quickly. Wash brushes when they're not in use.

3 *Priming the body*

Bottoms up. Whatever the type of furniture, from chairs to hutches to tables, start priming the body of the piece of furniture from the bottom. Lay chests and cabinets on their backs and turn chairs and tables upside-down. (If the furniture is heavy, get some help lifting it.) Using a brush, cut-in all corners and places that are inaccessible with a roller. Then roller paint the primer up to the brushwork on all surfaces that you can comfortably reach. Priming the backs and interiors of cabinets, desks and dressers is optional.

Stand the piece upright. Cut-in and roller paint all remaining surfaces. Wash all paint utensils with soap and warm water. Allow the primer to dry.

4 *Painting*

Repeat steps 1 and 2, now using latex paint. Allow to dry and apply a second coat if necessary.

5 *Varnishing and finishing*

Continue, painting and decorating your piece of furniture, or if the piece is to be left a solid color, protect the paint and enrich the color by applying a non-yellowing, water-based varnish. (See *Varnishing,* page 48.)

Attach the hardware.

Binding may occur where paint comes into contact with other paint. In such areas, apply one or two heavy coats of paste wax and buff.

Paint the hardest-to-get-at areas first. There'll be less paint on the painter and more on the furniture.

Brush Painting

In spite of the numerous advances in paint tools and products, the most necessary and versatile tool is still the paint brush. But don't get caught up in brushmania. It's not necessary to buy an arsenal of expensive brushes for painting furniture. Use a medium-width brush with an angled cut to the bristles for cutting-in and for painting flat sections; an artist's square-tipped brush for narrow areas and detail work; and a fine-point artist's brush for freehand, intricate painting. While full-coverage painting is usually executed with a combi-

Creating with a brush adds individuality and personality to an otherwise straightforward paint treatment.

nation of brush and roller, sometimes brush painting is necessary to produce brushstrokes, desirable in many antiquing and rustic treatments. (See *Painting Tools*, page 24; *Specialty Products*, page 32.)

There is no foolproof way to achieve a perfect paint job with a brush. There are, however, approaches to brush painting that will garner a smoother, more even coat with fewer drips and sags. Purchasing good-quality brushes, made to be used with your type of paint, either oil- or water-based, is a good start.

MATERIALS

The following tools and materials may be required.

- quart (litre) eggshell or satin finish latex paint in the color of your choice
- paint brush, 1½ in. (4 cm) wide, for water-based paint
- tube of acrylic paint in the color of your choice
- artist's brushes, medium square-tipped or fine point
- chalk or colored pencil

1 *Brush painting a flat area*

Stir the latex paint. Dip the paint brush into the paint to a level of about one-third to one-half of the bristles. Drag one side of the bristles against the lip of the can when removing the brush from the can.

Lay the wet side of the brush on an open part of the furniture, inside an edge. Brush the paint outward, brushing the length of the area, not the width.

Brush toward and over edges, if possible. If the brush is dragged against an edge, as shown in the photo, the paint will form drips.

Continue brushing, quickly and deftly smoothing the paint. Reload the brush as needed. Keep a constant watch for drips, swiping them away with the brush. Water-based paint sets quickly. Avoid brushing over the same area several times.

Overbrushing will create deep brush-strokes in the setting paint. Finish painting one section of the piece at a time.

2 *Cutting-in*

When painting joins and corner detail, load a small amount of paint onto the brush and use the longer point of the brush's angled tip to coax paint into the corner, dragging the brush alongside the join. The angled cut on the brush suits this technique, especially when cutting-in on the insides of drawers and other pieces with many angles and inside corners. Watch for drips and sags, swiping them away with the brush.

3 *Painting details*

Though spray paint is usually best for spindles and other ornamental work, sometimes details must match the overall effect of a brush-painted piece. Load the brush with a small amount of paint. Holding the brush on an angle, drag it in a downward motion along the spindle, depositing the paint in a long bead.

Quickly brush out the paint to an even coat. Watch for any drips and sags, brushing them out.

4 *Freehand brushwork*

Freehand painting in contrasting colors is attractive on carved or turned details. Position at eye level the area to be painted. Use an artist's brush of a size suitable for the area, and artist's acrylics or latex paint. Thin the paint if needed so that it flows easily from the brush, but is not watery. Try to maintain a steady hand. Keep edges even and end the color at a natural break.

To paint freehand designs, such as curlicues or trailing vines, draw your design first with a piece of chalk or a colored pencil. Use a fine-point artist's brush and acrylic or latex paint, thinned if necessary to flow from the brush. Dip the point of the brush into the paint. With your hand raised (laying the heel of your hand on the table creates cramped shapes), apply pressure on the brush to obtain the thickness of the line desired. Paint the line, using the chalk line as a guide only. Following the chalk line too closely will cause hesitation, resulting in tentative lines.

Rollers are available in a wide variety of sizes.
Choose one that fits the job.

Roller Painting

The roller is undoubtedly one of the most important painting tools, second only to the paint brush. It provides fast, even coverage and smooth texture without brushstrokes. A relatively recent invention, the roller has revolutionized painting. But until recently, roller painting was viewed only as a fast way to cover large areas. New, creative ways of using this versatile tool are now being explored to produce repetitive patterns and textured layering of color. For painting furniture, purchase a small roller handle with removable short-pile sleeves to fit. Buy two or

The smooth texture of a roller-painted surface provides an excellent base for treatments such as sponging.

more sleeves, because most are good for only one application of paint. Choose a paint tray to fit the roller. A paint tray is better than a paper plate or other disposable substitutes, because its reservoir and textured ramp provide more even distribution and better control of the paint. First, with a brush, cut-in on far corners and other hard-to-get-at places. Then use the roller to apply primer or paint, but not varnish. Varnish should always be brushed on.

MATERIALS

The following tools and materials may be required.

- quart (litre) eggshell or satin finish latex paint in the color of your choice
- roller handle, 4 in. (10 cm) wide, and short-pile sleeves to fit
- roller tray to fit roller
- fine sandpaper (220 grade or finer), tack cloth

1 *Ready to roll*

To prevent air bubbles from forming in the paint and to remove any loose roller-sleeve lint, dampen the sleeve and rub it as dry as possible with a paper towel.

Pour paint into the reservoir of the tray, filling it about half full. Dip the roller sleeve into the tray and roll it so that the full sleeve is coated in paint.

Roll excess paint from the roller on the ramp of the tray, but don't overdo it. The roller should still hold a good quantity of paint.

2 *Applying an even coat*

Position the roller on a surface of the furniture, inside the edges. Beginning at this central point, roll the paint outward in a triangular fashion, criss-crossing previous lines. This technique will give even texture and prevent a grid from appearing. Don't try to achieve full coverage in only one coat. Excessive paint that isn't rolled out will create stretch marks – an undesirable texture.

Apply moderate, even pressure. Let the roller do the work. It is better to reload the roller with paint than to squeeze more paint from it. Heavy pressure will create railroad tracks – a double line of heavy paint formed along the sides of the roller.

3 *Roller logic*

Roll toward and over edges, instead of pulling the roller against an edge. Rolling against an edge creates drips. As you roll, be on the lookout for drips and either swipe them with a brush or roll them out.

Continue rolling, overlapping each new roller of paint over the edge of the last, until the full surface is covered. Avoid the temptation to reroll a wet section. Water-based paint sets quickly, and rerolling will tear up the surface. Instead, allow to dry and apply another coat. For an ultrasmooth finish, lightly sand the first coat with fine sandpaper when it is completely dry and wipe clean with a tack cloth before applying the second coat. Between coats, keep paint wet by placing the tray and roller in a plastic bag, squishing the bag to eliminate air.

Block printing with a roller creates beautifully rendered, consistent, multiple prints for borders or all-over patterns, an ideal complement to an antiqued finish.

Be sure to check the direction of the nozzle.

Spray Painting

Spray painting gives smooth, dense coverage to furniture with ornamental carving and texture. The invasive nature of spray paint allows it to go where a brush can't reach, quickly and without drips or sags from brushing. Wherever you spray paint, large dropsheets are required to avoid home-and-garden decorating by default. Only a small portion of the paint coming from the nozzle connects with your furniture. The overspray really travels, settling on surfaces and in tiny crevices. So tape dropsheets together and cover everything that might catch drifting paint. Also make sure you work in a well-ventilated environment to avoid asphyxiating the canary. Spray painting outside is fine, unless it is too breezy. A garage with an open door is

The lacquerlike quality of spray paint provides the perfect ground for a creative, freehand treatment.

best. Indoors, several open windows, or an open window with a fan, will help. Inevitably, a certain amount of fumes and spray will be inhaled, simply because of the painter's proximity to the spray can. A paper mask will screen out spray paint particles, while a charcoal mask will filter out both paint and the fumes of the paint.

Most sprays don't require primer. But if your furniture has a patchy, uneven finish, spray with primer first. Acrylic-based sprays, available in both low-luster and glossy finishes, are superb for most furniture. Choose a specialty spray paint to cover rust or to add texture. If the local paint store has a limited selection of finishes or types of spray paint, try hardware outlets or art supply or craft stores.

MATERIALS

The following tools and materials may be required.

- dropsheets
- charcoal mask or painter's mask
- one or more cans of acrylic spray paint
- one or more cans of spray primer
- one or more cans of rust-covering spray paint
- steel-wool pad

1 *Getting started*

Attention allergy sufferers: a charcoal mask to eliminate fumes is recommended. If the label indicates flammable (inflammable) or explosive, do not work where there may be open flame, including a flame as tiny as the pilot light on a stove, furnace or water heater.

Using plastic dropsheets, old bedsheets or paper (not newspaper because the ink will transfer to the painted piece), cover every surface around your furniture piece that may catch some stray spray or overspray.

Shake the can for at least two full minutes. Test by spraying paint on a piece of paper. The first few sprays may appear watery until the paint makes its way up the tube.

2 *Spray primer*

If you use a primer, apply one coat. Primer dries very fast. You should be able to turn the piece of furniture as you work, spraying all surfaces quickly. Allow to dry thoroughly.

3 *Rust-covering spray paint*

If using a special rust-covering spray paint, remove as much rust as possible from the furniture with water and a steel-wool pad. Rinse well and allow to dry. Follow the directions on the label for application and drying times.

4 *Spray painting, phase 1*

Position the piece of furniture upside-down on the dropsheet. (If the furniture is heavy, get some help lifting it.) Holding the can about 10 in. (25 cm) away from the object, depress the nozzle fully, spraying the furniture with a light, even coat. Spraying too heavily will create drips and sags. Several light coats are better than one heavy one. Spray all visible surfaces without moving the piece.

Recoat while the piece is in the same position. Check the label. The recoating instructions on most spray paints say to apply another coat within one hour. If you miss that deadline, you must wait three days to recoat. Apply as many coats as required for dense, even coverage.

5 *Spray painting, phase 2*

Allow the paint to become dry to the touch. Turn the piece of furniture upright and repeat step 4. Continue until all surfaces are covered. Allow to dry thoroughly.

The most beautiful stains can come from unexpected sources.

Staining Wood

The opaque density of paint invites creativity, but don't overlook the effect of stain on bare wood. Simple and very fast to apply, stains appear dark in their liquid form, yet are transparent when they dry. But transparent doesn't mean invisible. Stain not only provides color. As it is absorbed into the wood, it also accentuates the grain and markings. What was a bland, bare piece of pine five minutes ago is now a fascinating and intricate natural work of art. Most commercial stains for wood are natural brown wood shades. However,

A paint treatment such as freehand painting with crackle-varnish accentuates the mellow warmth of stained wood.

dramatic jewel tones, rustic colors or rich shades can be had from berries or fabric dyes.

After applying a commercial stain, protect the surface with wax, oil or varnish. Many stains are available already mixed with varnish or oil – making staining and finishing a one-step process. Ask at your paint store about these mixes. Always varnish natural or bright-colored stains to protect the finish and prevent transfer of color.

MATERIALS

The following tools and materials may be required.

- commercial stain in an appropriate quantity
- fine sandpaper (180 to 220 grade)
- sanding block
- tack cloth
- small quantity of white shellac or other sealer

- wooden stir stick
- paint brush
- rags
- quart (litre) non-yellowing, water-based varnish; or furniture oil or wax and buffing cloth

1 *Getting started*

Start with completely bare wood, free of paint, varnish or glue. If the wood was previously painted and stripped it must be free of all paint residue, and the surface should be lightly sanded to open the grain. Unpainted wooden furniture is often sealed – the result of saws used to cut the wood – giving the wood a slightly shiny surface. Wood that is sealed will absorb stain unevenly, giving the surface a patchy appearance. Sand unpainted furniture lightly with fine sandpaper to open the grain.

Holding the sandpaper flat in your hand or using a sanding block, sand the surface lightly with fine sandpaper in the direction of the grain. (Sanding across the grain can create deep scratches.) Wipe the surface clean with a tack cloth.

End cuts – where the wood is cut across the grain – may absorb a large quantity of stain, becoming darker than the rest of the furniture. If you don't want this effect, dilute some white shellac or other sealer to half its normal strength and brush it onto the open grain. When the sealer is dry, stain the edge.

Using a wooden stir stick, stir the stain thoroughly. Wipe the stick on a rag and double check the color of the stain on the stick.

2 *Applying stain*

Lay the surface to be stained in a horizontal position to prevent runs. (If the furniture is heavy, get help lifting it.) Dip a brush or a rag into the stain and begin to spread the stain onto the wood. Most of the stain will be absorbed.

Follow the fresh stain with a clean rag, wiping away excess. Continue staining and wiping the excess, staining to the wet edge of the previous section.

When the full side is stained, allow to dry. Then turn it over and stain the other side. Continue until all sides of the piece are stained.

3 *Protecting the finish*

The finish of a stained piece must be protected. When the stained surfaces are dry, protect them by varnishing, oiling or waxing. Consult your paint store about the different applications available.

Clear thinking: Varnish in a dust-free setting.

Varnishing

Varnishing not only protects your paint job from scuffing, chipping and the effects of cleaning compounds. It also enriches color and gives a deep, glasslike finish. Some fragile materials such as paper and fabric, when protected by several coats of varnish, can be used in unexpected and creative ways. While it's best to apply varnish over an entire piece of furniture, you may opt to varnish only the parts that receive the most wear and need the greatest protection, such as a tabletop or the drawer fronts of a dresser.

Select a non-yellowing, water-based varnish in your choice of finish, from low luster to glossy. These varnishes are fast drying, skinning over within minutes, a quality that helps prevent dust from becoming embedded in the surface. Water-based varnishes have a relatively slight odor and are easy to

Applying water-based varnish is like wrapping furniture in plastic, making delicate dried leaves tough and durable.

clean up with soap and water.

There are only two rules for achieving water-based varnish perfection. First, do it fast, quickly "floating" the varnish onto the surface with a brush, never a roller. Second, resist the urge to touch. Varnish begins to set immediately, and brush marks, fingerprints and kitty's paw prints are permanent. When the varnish is dry (usually a few hours), sand the finish lightly with fine sandpaper, wipe clean with a tack cloth and apply another coat. Don't be alarmed by the cloudy effect sanding has on the varnish. It will disappear when the next coat is applied.

Occasionally, a project with a special treatment, such as crackled varnish, will call for an oil-based varnish. These varnishes take much longer to dry than water-based ones, overnight compared with a few hours. They also lend an amber tone to the finish.

MATERIALS

The following tools and materials may be required.

- easy-release painter's tape
- tack cloth
- quart (litre) non-yellowing, water-based varnish

- paint brush, 2 in. (5 cm) wide, for water-based paint
- fine sandpaper (220 grade or finer)
- paste wax or car wax, buffing cloth

1 Getting started

Use easy-release painter's tape to mask around the area that you will varnish. Varnish must be stirred, never shaken. Shaking will create a multitude of bubbles that become trapped in the quickly drying varnish. While applying the varnish, stir it about every fifteen minutes.

2 Applying varnish

With a tack cloth, wipe the piece to be varnished, removing every particle of dust from the surface.

Using the paint brush, apply the first coat. Dip your brush to a level about halfway up the bristles.

Without wiping the excess off the brush, flow on a short, wide strip of varnish, starting near one corner or edge. Brush varnish out quickly and smoothly in the direction of the length of the surface, not the width. Try to brush toward the edges. Brushing against edges causes runs and drips.

Repeat, brushing a second wide strip beside the first and connecting the strips. Continue until a section is complete. As you work, check for varnish that has slopped over edges and is creating drips. Wipe drips away with a brush, rag or finger. Continue across the surface, adding to the wet edge of previous strokes, until the surface is covered. Wash out the brush with soap and warm water.

Have a cup of tea and allow the varnish to dry.

3 Additional coats

When the varnish is thoroughly dry (usually about a couple of hours), sand the first coat lightly with fine sandpaper and wipe thoroughly with a tack cloth. The cloudy effect that the sanding has on the varnish will disappear when you apply the next coat.

Apply a second coat. Allow to dry. Sand again and apply a third coat, if desired.

Optional: Applying and buffing a coat of paste wax or car wax over the last, dry coat of varnish will produce a glowing, buttery finish.

Crackled varnish is created by layering gum Arabic over tacky oil-based varnish. The resulting cracks are highlighted by rubbed-in oil paint.
(See The Cupboard Was Bare, page 102.)

Cupboard Love

A TRADITIONAL QUEBEC TREATMENT
FOR AN UNUSUAL FOLK ART CUPBOARD

Judging from the elegant inset arches on each panel, this interesting cabinet
appears to have been assembled from a collection of old church doors.
Used as a garage storage cupboard it lost its grandeur as well as its floor,
and gained many mouse- and ant-sized cracks. Painting and antiquing the
cabinet in traditional Quebec colors disguises its flaws and accentuates
its elegant lines while keeping its folk integrity intact. Some of the
cracks were left, adding to the piece's farmhouse charm.
The overall effect is sturdy and rustic.

Read This First

The paint-and-antiquing technique demonstrated on this armoire can be applied to any piece of furniture – as long as the piece is made from solid wood, not particleboard or melamine. Unpainted furniture pieces are ideal for this treatment. If the piece is already painted, you will need to decide whether the existing color will work with your treatment. If it won't, you'll need to strip it partially or fully because areas will be sanded back to expose the undercoating. If the piece is varnished, sand it with a fine sandpaper or degloss the surface with TSP (see *Deglossing Agents,* page 18) for better paint adhesion.

BEFORE

A folk art cupboard? This neglected piece had varnish weathered to the wood, no floor and no feet. And in spite of its heavy weight and the thickness of the wood, it wobbled impressively. Strategic shoring with cut-and-nailed two-by-fours solved the disintegrating feeling and got it off the ground.

MATERIALS

- sandpaper or TSP deglossing compound, wood filler, scraper, other wood-repair materials and tools
- paint brush, 2 in. (5 cm) wide
- quart (litre) low–luster finish latex paint, barn red
- quart (litre) low–luster finish latex paint, deep linen blue
- medium and fine sandpaper (120 and 220 grades)
- amber stain
- rags
- paste wax, buffing cloth
- *optional:* rubber gloves

1 *Getting started*

Repair the piece, filling any cracks or holes as needed. (See *Preparation,* page 36.)

Sand or wash with TSP to degloss the surface for painting. If necessary, strip the piece to expose raw wood, as needed for the antiquing process (step 4). This cabinet was originally varnished, although most of the varnish had worn off. It was washed with TSP to clean the surface and degloss all remaining varnish.

Note: For photography purposes, the door was not removed from the cabinet. For best results, remove doors, drawers, etc., and paint separately.

2 *Painting the base coat*

Do not paint the cabinet with primer. Using the barn red paint and a brush (brushstrokes are desirable with this technique), paint the entire exterior of the cabinet, getting as much coverage as possible with one coat of paint. (See *Brush Painting,* page 40.) A second coat is not necessary, even if the first coat is not fully opaque. Paint the inside if desired. Allow to dry.

Though only some of the red will be exposed later, in the antiquing process, it is important to paint the full exterior. Eventually more aging will occur, and the red paint will show through the wear spots.

3 *Painting the top coat*

Using a brush, paint over the red paint with deep linen blue. Allow to dry. This color should be solid. Apply a second coat, if necessary.

4 *Antiquing*

When the paint is dry to the touch, use a medium-grade sandpaper to sand through the layers of paint. Sand wherever you feel natural wear will occur, exposing areas of red paint and some wood. Usually, wear occurs on all corners, on the high spots of trim and wherever a door or drawer would be pushed or pulled for opening and closing. Finish with a fine sandpaper.

5 *Staining*

Using a rag, apply amber stain to all areas of raw wood that have been exposed by the sanding. Wax and buff the stained areas with paste wax.

Attach the hardware.

Crackle

AGING ARTFULLY
WITH A SIMPLE RECIPE FOR CRACKLE

Crackle is reminiscent of weathered barns and farmhouse kitchens.
Like pouring time from a bottle, applying this technique creates instant
antiques. Furniture treated to a crackle finish (also called crackleure)
immediately takes on a convincingly aged and distressed look. This time-worn,
rural treatment of overlaid and crackled traditional colors, accented by simple
potato block-printing, holds its own in any rustic setting.

Read This First

There are two types of crackle. One type has the effect of severely weathered paint. In the other, only the varnish is crazed into spiderweb-like cracks, while the underlying paint is intact. This project demonstrates the weathered-paint type of crackle. (For the second type, see *The Cupboard Was Bare,* page 102, steps 8 and 9.) Pass over the pricey crackle kits sold in paint, art supply and craft stores. The inexpensive foolproof method demonstrated here creates incredibly authentic-looking crackle, quickly. To produce the crackle, a base-coat color of latex paint is applied to the furniture. If your cabinet has a plastic laminate finish, use melamine paint for the base coat. (See *Melamine Paint,* page 27.) This color will show through the cracks. Mucilage glue is brushed on over the paint. Then, while the glue is still wet, a coordinating top coat of paint is applied. This top coat will begin cracking within minutes. Latex-based paint cracks much more effectively than acrylic-based paint, although a latex-acrylic blend can be used. For this cabinet, strongly contrasting colors of paint were used to demonstrate the effect dramatically. Similar colors crackled overtop each other produce a subtle, intricate result.

Potato printing is a perfect complement for crackle. Potato prints are by nature simple and imperfect, uneven and semitransparent, with an aged look. Potato printing is as simple as it sounds — stamping with a cut-out potato, like a rubber stamp. Crackle, because it is so busy, can often obscure proportions and details. Potato printing or block printing accentuates details and restores order.

BEFORE

An intriguing cabinet of plank construction with a garage paint job of dull cement gray. Crackle and block printing will accentuate its 1920s vintage and its handsome proportions.

MATERIALS

- latex paint in two coordinating colors, 1 quart (litre) each (Choose a low-luster finish for authenticity.)
- mucilage glue, the amber type used in grade school (One bottle will cover a surface just larger than two of these books lying open.)
- inexpensive medium-sized paint brush (for glue)
- paint brush, 2 in. (5 cm) wide
- paper, pencil, scissors
- large potato
- sharp paring knife
- medium-sized artist's brush
- tubes of acrylics for potato print: cadmium red deep, mars black, yellow ochre
- ruler or tape measure

1 Painting the base coat

Refer to *Painting Basics* (page 34), and prepare and paint (priming is not necessary) the cabinet with the base-coat color. Apply two coats if necessary to achieve good coverage. This is the color that will show through the cracks. Allow the paint to dry. Place the area to be crackled in a horizontal position. (If the cabinet is heavy, get help moving it.) Decant some mucilage glue into a container.

2 Applying crackle

Apply the crackle in sections about 2 square feet (.2 m square). Using a medium-sized paint brush, spread the mucilage on the surface, brushing it out to a thin layer. The crackle will occur naturally along the direction of the brushstrokes. For busy, intricate crackle, brush in overlapping, multiple directions. Brush in straight lines for more even crackle. Place brush in glue and set aside.

Without allowing the mucilage to dry, use the 2 in. (5 cm) paint brush and brush the second color of paint over the wet mucilage, almost to the edges of the glue. Flow the paint on without overbrushing. The largest crackles will be formed on the wettest glue, with the size of crackles diminishing as the paint is applied over damp glue. No crackles will be formed on dry glue.

Paint another section of glue, overlapping the still-wet edges of the first section, and apply more paint over the wet glue. Continue until the full side is covered. Cracking will start in minutes. Allow the side to dry. Continue crackling the cabinet until all sides are finished.

3 Cutting the potato print

Trace the pattern on page 59, or create your own pattern.

Cut a large potato in half, lengthwise. Cut out the design elements of the pattern and position them on the cut side of the potato-half. Trace around the pattern pieces with a pencil or a felt pen. (Retain the other potato-half.)

Using a sharp paring knife, cut away the potato surrounding the pattern outlines to a depth of about ¼ in. (.5 cm) or greater. On the uncarved side of the potato, carve two notches as a handle.

4 Potato printing

Using a medium-sized artist's brush, apply acrylics, in the desired colors, to the raised sections of the potato. (Shown here: cadmium red deep, mars black, and yellow ochre.)

It's a good idea to do some test prints on paper before printing the cabinet. Carefully position the potato print, paint-side-down, onto the paper. Apply pressure so that the print makes full contact. Carefully lift the potato print off without sliding it. The print should be uneven and semitransparent, and it may have gaps.

Now place the surface to be printed in a horizontal position, so that you can apply pressure. Begin printing the cabinet, forming a border or a center design.

Continue printing with the potato, replenishing paint as needed, about every two or three prints. When finished, stand back and examine the prints. You can touch up any gaps or areas that are too transparent for your taste. Patting the paint on with a brush or your finger gives a block-printing effect.

5 *Sawtooth border*

To create a block-printed sawtooth border, cut an equilateral triangle (Geometry 101: all sides equal length) from the other potato-half. Measure and mark the center of the border. Apply mars black paint to the potato.

Position the first print on the center of the border, where marked. Work out from the center, with triangles just touching, until one edge of the border is complete.

Continue the border along adjoining sides, if desired.

Optional: Paint small motifs or dots in the open Vs of the sawtooth.

Attach the hardware.

PATTERN FOR POTATO PRINT

For a more subtle, refined look than crackled paint, try creating crackled, antiqued varnish. (See The Cupboard Was Bare, page 102.)

Country Folk

A COUNTRY CHAIR IS CHARMED WITH DECORATIVE, EFFORTLESS HAND PAINTING

Not just any old chair, this sturdy, solid wooden one, with its turned spindles and legs and its subtly decorative backrest, elicits a simple, homey feeling. It was probably part of a kitchen set but, judging by the saw grooves, nicks and gouges, ended up as a workshop chair. First made with a natural wood finish, it was later painted off-white. This became its original paint. Original paint is considered untouchable by many antique aficionados — part of the furniture's history. Like many absolutes, this one must be tempered by reality. The owner of this chair wanted it repainted to suit her rustic yet refined decor.

Read This First

This project is quick and straightforward. First the chair is painted a solid deep-green base coat, either by spray painting or by brush. If your chair has a plastic laminate finish, use melamine paint for the base coat. (See *Melamine Paint,* page 27.) Then, with the help of templates, the floral pattern is applied. Templates look like stencil cut-outs, but instead of filling the cut-out areas with paint, you use them to trace an outline that's then filled in by brush painting. Stencils tend to give a smooth, even texture, while this technique achieves a hand-painted look with the brush-strokes and subtleties that give brushwork its appeal. Patterns for templates are provided on page 64. If the chair is wooden, you may wish to antique the paint. (See *Cupboard Love,* page 50.)

BEFORE

Lots of country character. The chair could be left as is, preserving its rustic and historic integrity, or painted in a style that complements its old world flavor.

MATERIALS

- can of low-luster acrylic spray paint, or quart (litre) satin finish latex paint, deep green
- 1½ in. (4 cm) wide paint brush (if using latex paint)
- paper, pen, scissors; access to photocopier
- white chalk or pencil crayon
- tubes of acrylic paint: cadmium red deep, yellow oxide, green gold, Prussian blue
- oval-tipped artist's brush, medium width
- fine-point artist's brush
- *optional:* can of spray primer or quart (litre) brush-on, water-based primer (The patchy finish of this chair required priming.)
- *optional:* medium and fine sandpaper (120 and 220 grades)
- *optional:* pint (.5 litre) non-yellowing, water-based varnish, or can of spray varnish

1 *Painting the base coat*

Following the instructions for *Preparation* (page 36), prepare the chair.

If the finish of the chair is patchy, paint the chair with one coat of primer, either by spraying or brushing it on. (See *Brush Painting,* page 40; or *Spray Painting,* page 44.)

If the chair is wooden and you wish to antique it, don't prime it. (See *Cupboard Love,* page 50.)

Spray paint or brush on two coats of deep green.

2 *Using templates*

Trace the patterns (page 64) onto paper, using a photocopier to enlarge or reduce them, if necessary, to the size appropriate for your chair. Cut out the centers of the templates, reserving the outer portion.

Lay the *Large Tulip* template onto the seat of the chair and run chalk or pencil crayon around the inside edge. Repeat three times, making a four-square pattern of tulips in the center of the seat. Draw symmetrical branches freehand, starting between the tulip shapes at the top and bottom and ending near the corners.

Draw smaller symmetrical branches between the tulip shapes at the sides.

Using the *Medium Tulip* template, trace flowers at each corner. Using the *Small Tulip* template, trace small flowers at the sides.

Using the same templates, draw a design onto both sides of the backrest of the chair. Especially pleasing is a design of tulips at the center, with branches extending to the sides.

3 *Hand painting*

Paint in the tulip outlines on the seat and both sides of the backrest with the oval-tipped brush and cadmium red deep paint. This job may require two coats.

Using the fine-point artist's brush and the yellow oxide, paint yellow centers onto the four-square tulips and the side tulips. Add lines to separate the petals, and create dots for stamens. Don't forget the backrest.

Using the green gold, paint lines along the chalk lines for the branches. Don't expect to follow the lines exactly. They are only a guide. Create small oval leaves by pressing the side of the fine-point brush against the surface.

With the Prussian blue, paint bunches of dots for a decorative element (like buds), where desired. You may also wish to add a decorative border of blue half-circles and dots. (Plan the border first, by sketching it with chalk.) Prussian blue can also be used to accentuate the edges of the branches and leaves.

Add these same elements to the backrest.

4 *Painting spindles*

Using any combination of colors, paint the spindles of the chair, keeping the edges as even as possible. (See *Brush Painting,* page 40.)

If you wish to antique your chair, sand wear spots onto it. (See *Cupboard Love,* page 50.) This can be done only on wooden chairs that have not been primed before painting.

5 *Varnishing*

Optional: Enrich the color and protect your paint job. Varnish the seat and backrest with two coats of non-yellowing, water-based varnish. Or use spray varnish to varnish the full chair. (See *Varnishing,* page 48.)

TEMPLATES FOR SEAT AND BACKREST

Large Tulip

Medium Tulip

Small Tulip

The floral motif which was used on our chair has a Central European flavor. For a softer, less structured effect, block prints, which are sold at craft stores, can be used with translucent glazes.

Tabletop Rose Bower

MISTY ROSE STENCILS BEDECK
A WOODEN TABLE

Step into a pastel-painted Victorian rose garden. This impressionistic paint
treatment is nostalgically English country and reminiscent of a turn-of-the-
century lady's hatbox, with its hand-painted florals bordered by stripes and
sprinkled with tiny blossoms. This adaptable table moves easily
into an entryway or a bathroom, kitchen or bedroom.

Read This First

Choose furniture with an English-cottage feeling: simple wooden pieces with some trim, turned legs, or other gentle but not fussy detail. First, the table is painted with a solid base coat of latex paint. If your table has a plastic laminate finish, use melamine paint for the base coat. (See *Melamine Paint,* page 27.) Then flat areas are sponge painted and stenciled with rose and leaf motifs. A solid wood piece finished in this style can be antiqued if it is not primed before painting. (See *Cupboard Love,* page 50.) If pastels are too intense for your color scheme, step 7 shows how to apply a glaze over the paint for a muted look. Or try working in Victorian sepia tones of burgundy, slate blue and taupe. Four different stencils are used in this project, with many being layered. (Patterns are on page 71.) Choose acrylics or the cream paints made for stenciling. Acrylic paints are preferred for their fast drying times. If you use the cream stencil paints available in craft stores, expect each color to take several days to dry.

MATERIALS

- quart (litre) high-adhesion, water-based primer (or spray primer)
- quart (litre) eggshell finish latex paint, powder blue
- painting tools: paint brush, small roller, roller tray
- synthetic or natural sponge for sponge painting
- for sponging: latex and/or acrylic paints – pastel pink, pastel blue-green, off-white
- stencil plastic (available at art supply and craft stores (or lightweight cardboard))
- scissors or X-acto knife
- pink colored pencil
- for stenciling: tubes of acrylics (and an inexpensive square-tipped artist's brush), or cream stencil paints (and a stencil brush) – acid green, pastel blue-green, pastel pink, medium pink
- for hand painting: tubes of acrylics – yellow, off-white, deep blue, medium green, dark blue-gray
- fine-point artist's brush and medium-sized artist's brush
- easy-release painter's tape or masking tape
- quart (litre) non-yellowing, water-based varnish
- *optional:* spray glue; scrap paper, dropsheets

BEFORE

A pleasantly proportioned 1940s wooden table with turned spindle legs and gingerbread trim. When the flaking varnish is scraped down and the legs and trim are repaired, it becomes the perfect foil for a Victorian treatment.

1 *Painting*

Refer to *Painting Basics* (page 34). Prepare, prime and paint the table with two coats of powder blue paint.

Allow to dry. If you wish to antique the table, do not prime it. (See *Cupboard Love*, page 53.)

2 *Sponge painting*

Mix each of the colors listed for sponging.

Use easy-release painter's tape or masking tape to mask off the area to be sponge painted.

Mix the pastel pink paint with water to a soupy consistency, or add glaze. (See *Glaze,* page 28.) Tear off a chunk of sponge and dampen it slightly with water. Then saturate it with paint. Squeeze out most of the paint.

Using a pouncing motion, sponge the tabletop (and any other sections that you wish), leaving about half the blue showing through. Make the coverage in some spots heavier, to resemble cloud formations. The base coat (powder blue) will begin disappearing, with each subsequent sponged-on color gaining prominence.

3 *Sponge painting, continued*

While the pink paint is still damp, sponge paint over it with pastel blue-green, allowing both pink and blue to show through.

Sponge paint a final coat of off-white, allowing the previous colors to glow through. Allow to dry.

4 *Preparing stencils*

While the sponge painting is drying, trace the rose and leaf patterns onto the stencil plastic (or similar material) and cut out the center shaded areas. The cutting can be done with scissors or an X-acto knife.

For easier stenciling, spray-glue the backs of the stencils. Let the glue dry at least an hour to a light tackiness. (If the glue is too sticky, it will lift the background paint.)

Try a few test stencils on paper before stenciling the table. Press the stencil onto paper and, using an artist's paint brush or a stencil brush (a round brush with stiff bristles and a flat end), paint the center of the stencil. A paint brush will give a hand-painted look with brushstrokes, while the stencil brush will give smooth color. Add freehand lines or details.

5 Stenciling

Using the *Rose in Bloom* stencil and a pink colored pencil, mark the positions of roses on the table. Set this stencil aside.

Using the *Large Leaf* stencil and acid green paint, stencil leaves around and overlapping the marked roses. Lay the stencil onto the surface, gently pressing it down for adhesion. Then paint the full opening to all edges. Carefully lift the stencil while the paint is still wet, and proceed to the next leaf. Be careful not to lay the stencil over wet paint. It's advisable first to stencil in corners of the table, adding more leaves in between as the paint dries.

Using the *Small Leaf* stencil and the pastel blue-green paint, stencil leaves adjoining the large leaves. Allow them to overlap the large leaves in some places, and in other places stop at the outline of the large leaves.

Using the *Rose in Bloom* stencil and pastel pink, stencil the roses where you marked them, covering parts of some leaves and painting around others.

Using the *Center Rose* stencil and the medium-pink paint, stencil centers on top of the roses. The centers can be stenciled on the roses in any direction. There is no particular way they must be lined up.

6 Hand painting

Mix a small amount of yellow into some off-white paint. Using a medium-sized artist's brush, paint random highlights onto the roses.

Paint short, curved outline strokes in and around the roses, using the deep-blue paint and a fine-point artist's brush. Paint random shadows and center lines onto the leaves, using a medium green and a fine-point artist's brush.

Create clusters of small dots in among the roses, using the dark-blue-gray paint and a fine-point artist's brush.

Paint the spindles on the legs, or add other details such as stripes, as shown here, with colors of your choice.

7 *Varnishing and glazing*

Enrich color and protect the paint by varnishing with non-yellowing, water-based varnish. If the colors are stronger than desired, glaze them to reduce their intensity by adding a very small amount of off-white paint to the varnish, mixing thoroughly. Brush onto the table as you would with pure varnish. (See *Varnishing,* page 48.)

STENCIL PATTERNS

Rose in Bloom

Center Rose

Large Leaf

Small Leaf

Keeping Time

A CHARMING ROCKER REVEALS ITS PASTEL-PAINTED PAST

An old chair such as this well-worn rocker, or another piece of furniture with many layers of paint, can be refurbished imaginatively. Impressionist painters created radiant color by allowing layers of paint to glow through one another in a technique called *scumbling*. A similar quality is created in reverse by removing layers and partial layers of existing paint to produce a beautiful layered effect that reveals the furniture's history. In refurbishing the seat, the unexpected touch of woven wicking, normally used for oil lamps, adds texture and a neutral foil for the stripped paint.

Read This First

A piece of furniture with carved detail, clogged and obscured by layers of old paint, defies repainting. Painting over the drips and sags of a poor paint job guarantees another poor paint job. By stripping the piece only partially, you can eliminate lumps and bumps and reveal some of the furniture's history without the tedious finishing that stripping down to wood involves. Does stripping paint conjure up visions of vats of steaming toxic waste? Banish that image. You can now find new non-toxic, low-odor paint strippers.

The hand-crafted quality of a cane seat can be very attractive. If the cane is broken, however, that seat is a hazard and should be replaced. If you don't want the expense of recaning, try repairing the seat with webbing or with woven cotton wicking used in oil lamps. (See *Woven Seat,* page 129.)

BEFORE

Passed through many hands — most holding a paint brush — a small nursing rocker displays its last owner's handiwork: white oil-based enamel with nail polish hearts.

MATERIALS

- paint scraper
- newspaper; plastic dropsheet or old bedsheet
- rubber gloves
- low-toxicity paint stripper (Try to purchase a gel stripper.)
- inexpensive paint brush
- plastic stripping sponge
- fine sandpaper (220 grade)
- pint (.5 litre) acrylic or latex paint, in a color to suit your chair
- rags
- pint (.5 litre) non-yellowing, water-based varnish
- *optional:* tape and sheets of paper and plastic (for protecting the cane seat)
- *optional:* small hand saw or garden clippers (to remove cane seat)
- *optional:* plastic wrap, such as Saran wrap

1 *Seat preparation*

If you are planning to recane the seat, remove the old cane before doing anything else. A small hand saw or garden clippers are good for this surprisingly messy job. Cut as close to the rungs as possible and remove all pieces of cane that are wrapped around the rungs.

If you wish to retain the cane seat, protect it from the stripper by covering it in paper, then in a layer of plastic, taped securely closed.

If the chair has a cushion, unscrew it and remove it from the seat.

2 *Assessment*

Using a paint scraper or other sharp tool, scrape away a section of paint to investigate how many layers of paint there are and in what colors. You'll be better able to decide whether to partially strip and expose the layers, or to strip completely (and then stain or, possibly, repaint). (For more about complete stripping, see *The Cupboard Was Bare,* page 102.)

3 *Applying paint stripper*

Lay out several layers of newspaper covered with a large plastic, disposable dropsheet or an old bedsheet. Put on rubber gloves. Using the low-toxicity paint stripper and an inexpensive paint brush, paint one area of the chair with stripper.

Some strippers melt plastic. Try this test. Wrap the area in plastic wrap to prevent the stripper from running off. The plastic keeps the stripper in contact with the paint, making the stripping process faster and more even. If the stripper eats through the wrap, discontinue using the plastic. Continue until the whole chair is covered.

4 *Stripping paint*

When the top layer of paint is bubbled (the time can vary from fifteen minutes to an hour, depending on the brand of stripper), remove a section of plastic wrap. Remove loose paint with the paint scraper or scrub with the plastic stripping sponge to reveal the layers beneath.

The effect should be uneven, with various layers and some raw wood showing through in different places.

5 *Deactivating stripper*

Inspect the chair to determine which areas are satisfactory and which ones need to be stripped some more. Wash the satisfactory areas thoroughly with dish soap and water and rinse well to deactivate the stripper. Repeat and dry the surfaces with a rag.

Apply a second coat of stripper and plastic wrap to areas that require more stripping. Repeat step 4. Wash the stripped area. Allow the chair to dry. Some paint may remain soft. These areas will harden in time.

6 Sanding

Give the chair a light sanding with the fine sandpaper.

Inspect the chair. Don't be dismayed if it is mottled and blotchy looking. The next step will help even out the color.

7 Color washing

Choose a color of paint to suit the colors that have been revealed. Blue, rose or violet are good bets. Thin the paint with water to a watery consistency. Dip a small damp rag into the paint and wash the paint over a section of the chair.

Allow the paint to set slightly, only a minute or two. Then use a second clean, damp rag to wipe off some of the paint to the level of opacity you desire. Try not to obscure the scumbled, layered effect of the stripping.

Repeat the color washing over other sections.

To enrich color and protect the paint, apply one or two coats of non-yellowing, water-based varnish. (See *Varnishing,* page 48.)

If you wish to make a woven seat, see *Woven Seat,* page 129.

*If your chair has turned legs and spindles, painting the details in coordinating,
solid colors provides a decorative counterpoint to the soft washes of partial
stripping. (See Brush Painting, page 40.)*

Botanical Design

GRAPEVINES AND PRESSED LEAVES
PRODUCE A CRAFTED CABINET

Nothing creates style quite like the melding of a rich palette with the textures
and forms of nature. Earthy olive green paint and gray-stained natural wood
complement the controlled chaos of grapevines artfully arranged over
laminated, parchment-thin golden grape leaves. For a romantic effect, scatter
pressed flowers, petals and leaves over a soft pastel ground, or capture
autumn's fire with fall leaves on a richly hued background.

Read This First

Part of the pleasure of finishing this piece of furniture is the experience of finding and collecting leaves and vines. If grapevines are not available in your area, collect leaves that are a suitable shape and buy the vines from a florist or craft shop. Leaves must be pressed and dried for at least two weeks. If you do collect your own vines, do it in the summer or fall when the vines are pliable. Wear boots, long pants, and gloves – and watch out for poison ivy. Pull out good long lengths, the thicker the stem, the better. As you pull the vine down, wind and tie it into a coil, small enough to fit into a sink or laundry tub since the vines will later need soaking to rejuvenate them.

Collect leaves in the summer, if possible. By fall, grape leaves tend to be very fragile and thin. And fall colors aren't necessary because the leaves tend to change from green to a golden green-brown as they dry. While the leaves are drying, stain the cabinet's trim. Prime and paint the body with a base coat. If your armoire has a plastic laminate finish, use melamine paint for the base coat. (See *Melamine Paint, page 27.*)

BEFORE

An inexpensive unpainted wardrobe made of pine with very thin mahogany board panels can become a one-of-a-kind horticultural presence. All it needs are the right touches.

MATERIALS

- 2 dozen grape leaves
- scissors and a thick phone book
- 20 to 30 yd. (20 to 30 m) grapevines (allows for two vines on each side and two on the front, plus a generous portion for top arrangement)
- fine sandpaper (220 grade)
- pale- to medium-gray stain
- rag
- fine-point artist's brush
- easy-release painter's tape
- quart (litre) high-adhesion, water-based primer
- quart (litre) eggshell finish latex paint, deep olive green
- painting tools: paint brush, small roller, roller tray
- quart (litre) non-yellowing, water-based varnish
- paper towels
- carpet staples, small hammer
- garden clippers
- small quantity cellulose-based wallpaper paste

1 *Leaves*

Snip stems off the leaves and press them in a phone book. Leave about twenty pages between each page of leaves. Allow leaves to dry for at least two weeks.

2 *Vines*

Place a coil of vines in a bucket or sink and cover them with water. Soak the vines while the cabinet is being painted or for two hours.

3 *Staining trim*

Stain can be applied only to raw wood. (See *Staining Wood,* page 46.) Using fine sandpaper, lightly sand all areas that will be stained.

Remove doors and hardware. Place the doors on a tabletop and work on them while you work on the cabinet.

Stir the stain thoroughly. Using the artist's brush, apply stain along recessed trim or other hard-to-reach areas.

Using a rag or a paint brush, apply stain to the trim. Allow to dry.

4 *Painting panels*

Mask off all stained trim. Prime the panels and paint them with the deep olive green paint. (See *Painting Basics,* page 34.) Allow to dry.

Apply one coat of non-yellowing, water-based varnish to the stained areas of the armoire. Allow to dry, then repeat. Varnish can also be applied over the paint if desired. (See *Varnishing,* page 48.)

5 *Attaching vines*

Unwind the vines and pat them dry with paper towels. When the armoire is thoroughly dry, lay it on its side. (If the armoire is heavy, recruit a helper.) Starting at the bottom of the armoire, arrange the vines onto the uppermost side.

Starting at the bottom edge of the armoire, hammer carpet staples into the trim, anchoring the vine. Use as many staples as necessary to keep the vine reasonably close to the surface of the armoire.

Using garden clippers, cut the vine cleanly at the bottom edge of the armoire. Continue stapling the vine in place on the full side of the armoire. Don't cut off any excess vine at the top of the armoire.

Stand the armoire up (get help if needed) and arrange any trailing vines from the side along the top edge, stapling them in place. Don't allow them to hang in the door space. Otherwise, the door won't shut. Staple vines to the other side of the armoire and work any trailing vines into the top arrangement. Staple vines to the door panels, keeping them within the trim and working from a bottom corner to the opposite top corner.

6 *Laminating leaves*

Follow the instructions on the package of wallpaper paste to mix a small quantity.

Coat both sides of a leaf with the paste, leaving no dry spots.

Lay the leaf onto the surface of the armoire, aligning it with the vine. Smooth it from the center, eliminating any air pockets. Continue, pasting leaves on both sides of the armoire. The leaves may become wrinkly. The wrinkles will disappear as the leaves dry and shrink. Avoid trying to stretch the leaves flat. You will only damage the leaves.

7 *Doors*

Reattach the doors. Laminate leaves onto the doors. Allow both the vines and the leaves to dry.

8 *Varnishing*

Brush two coats of varnish over the leaves to protect them.

Branch management. If natural ingredients and rich colors are your preference, provide your wardrobe with hardware fashioned from twigs. (See Natural Tendencies, page 90.)

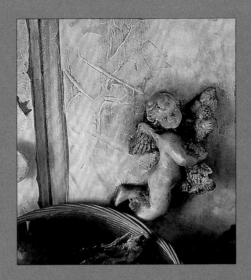

A Florentine Finish

WASHED IN STUCCO AND SEPIA, A PINE CUPBOARD TURNS CLASSIC TREASURE

Create a tiny corner of ancient Greece or Tuscany with faux stucco, washed in umber and sienna and enhanced by ornamental plaster garlands or seraphims. Ordinary materials and quick treatments combine for a neutral color scheme and historical mood on a dresser, cabinet or hutch.

Read This First

Choose a boxy wooden cabinet with some simple trim or molding. It should have planklike construction, rather than Victorian opulence. If applying this technique to a hutch or a dresser, be sure there is clearance around doors and drawers for them to close when coated with the faux stucco. Otherwise, limit the textured faux stucco treatment to the fronts of doors and drawers. Reserve this treatment for cabinets, dressers or hutches. The faux stucco may not stand up to the wear and tear of a tabletop.

The first stage of this treatment, the stucco effect, is accomplished with gesso, a thick white primer available at art supply and craft stores. The second stage, the antiquing, consists of brushing very liquid brown paint over the gesso, then wiping it off the high spots and allowing it to pool in the depressions. Shop for a chunky, aged-looking plaster angel or plaster fruit, often available at flower shops. Steer clear of the detailed Victorian variety sold at craft stores. A power drill is needed to attach the plaster embellishment.

BEFORE

Not well constructed and not well finished, this jam cupboard, made of pine, was serviceable but very plain. Pour on the texture.

MATERIALS

- quart (litre) gesso
- paint brushes
- easy-release painter's tape
- medium-width paint scraper
- medium sandpaper (180 grade)
- cans or other containers for support
- plaster figure or fruit
- 2 wood screws (long enough to go through the door and into the plaster figure)
- power drill
- white carpenter's glue
- tube of dark-brown acrylic paint (or substitute latex) for antiquing
- paper towel or rag
- *optional:* small wood chisel

1 *Getting started*

Repair and degloss your cabinet if necessary and remove hardware, drawers and doors. (See *Preparation*, page 36, in *Painting Basics*.)

The backboard was removed from this cabinet because it has a Colonial flavor.

2 *Priming*

Mask off any areas that you don't want faux stuccoed. Using a paint brush, paint the cabinet overall with a thin coat of gesso. This coat of gesso will act as a primer for better adhesion of the faux stucco layer. Allow to dry. Painting the interior is optional.

3 *Applying faux stucco*

Stucco one section of the cabinet at a time with the gesso. Begin with the door, laid flat on cans or other supports. Using the paint scraper, scoop a blob of gesso out of the container and plop it onto the surface of the door. Move the gesso around, folding it with the flat edge of the scraper, until the gesso is in textured layers.

Different widths of paint scrapers give different textures. As you work with the gesso, it will become thicker and the texturing will become easier.

Place the cabinet so that the side you're working on is horizontal, to prevent dripping. (If your cabinet is heavy, recruit help turning it.) Do one side of the cabinet at a time, allowing it to dry before turning it to do another side. Allow the entire cabinet to dry.

4 *Distressing news*

Using a small chisel or the scraper, distress the cabinet by rounding off sharp edges on the trim and on corners. Be careful! Digging too deeply can produce splinters that become larger as you go on. Small chunks can easily be chipped out of the surface as well. Using medium sandpaper, smooth any rough or splintered sections.

5 *Attaching the plaster figure*

Drill two leader-holes (narrower than the screws) into the back of the plaster figure, in the thickest section of the plaster.

With the door right-side-up, position the plaster figure on the center panel. Check that both the door and the figure are in line (right-way-up) by verifying that hinge holes in the door and the cabinet match. Keeping the figure in position, lift it slightly and mark the position of the two predrilled leader-holes onto the door.

Remove the figure and drill leader-holes through the door.

Apply white carpenter's glue in the area of the plaster figure. Position the figure onto the glue. Attach the wood screws from the wrong side of the door, through the door and into the plaster. Do not overtighten.

6 *Antiquing*

Antique one section of the cabinet at a time. Mix dark-brown acrylic or latex paint with water to a very liquid consistency. With a paint brush, wash paint onto a small area. Allow the paint to settle for about a minute.

Using a moist (not wet) paper towel or rag, wipe across the painted area, picking up paint in the high areas and leaving the

paint in depressions and hollows. This technique will emphasize the texture. The cabinet will take on an antique sepia tone, with crevices and any exposed wood a deep brown.

7 *Finishing*

Attach the hardware and the door. Touch up any hardware with gesso and, when it has dried, antique the hardware following the technique used in step 6.

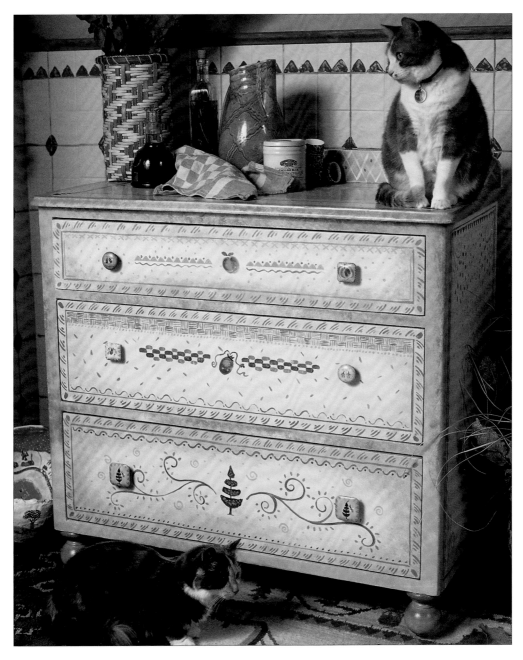

Texturing gives a country feel to furniture. Texturing can be achieved with paint and needn't be raised or bumpy. The sponge-painted borders of the dresser, above, soften the lines of the piece, making the freehand paint job warmer.

Natural Tendencies

BEDSTANDS GO COUNTRY WITH
NATURAL BRANCHES AND RICH COLOR

Bring the rustic indoors with natural tree branches — complete with bark, leaves and lichen — strategically installed as drawer pulls. Natural botanical properties such as leaves, twigs and branches lend personality and originality to furniture and accessories. Combined with rich traditional colors, these elements epitomize authentic style in country decorating. Antiquing is added for warmth and to soften the edges.

LET ME LIVE IN THE HOUSE
BY THE SIDE OF THE ROAD
AND BE A FRIEND TO MAN

Read This First

Painting, antiquing and adding the natural-branch drawer pulls are the basics of this project. The branches should be collected, and their ends sealed, at least two weeks before beginning this project, so they have a chance to dry. Use a small pruning saw or hand saw to cut the branches. Branches should be about the thickness of a broom handle – the more gnarly, the better. Cut the branches from a mature living tree. Fallen branches or branches from a dead tree will lose their bark and can split.

This treatment best suits a piece of wooden furniture that is simple with a rustic sensibility. A knock-down cabinet is easier to paint in several colors than is one already assembled. Feel free to paint the cabinet one color instead of three. If it has a plastic laminate finish, use melamine paint and a primer if indicated on the label. (See *Melamine Paint,* page 27.) To antique the cabinet as shown, it must be made of wood. Attaching the branches so that they are cut, yet appear to be in one piece, takes patience, determination and a power drill. But the results are well worth the effort. If working on two cabinets at once, as was done here, work on them at the same time, completing each step on both.

BEFORE

Knockdown furniture, like this two-drawer bedstand, offers a good opportunity for a multicolor paint job. No masking needed to separate colors, and none of the usual touch-ups required.

MATERIALS

- branches cut from a living tree (Using a small pruning saw or hand saw, cut more branches – and cut them longer – than you will need for the cabinet.)
- varnish or clear nail polish
- eggshell finish latex paint in three colors, 1 quart (litre) each: burgundy, navy blue, forest green
- paint brush, 2 in. (5 cm) wide
- plastic containers or boxes for support
- medium sandpaper (180 grade)
- chalk or colored pencil
- power drill
- wood screws
- *optional:* quart (litre) high-adhesion, water-based primer
- *optional:* amber stain, small rag
- *optional:* clamp or pliers

1 *Sealing branches*

Paint two coats of varnish or clear nail polish onto the cut ends of the branches. This will force the branches to dry slowly through the bark, instead of through the ends, preventing the wood from splitting and the bark from falling off. Allow the branches to dry for at least two weeks.

2 *Painting the body*

Assemble the body of the bedstand without the top. If you wish to paint the back, assemble it too. If not, leave it off.

If your bedstand is assembled, prepare the piece for painting. (See *Preparation,* page 36.)

If your bedstand is wooden and you wish to antique it, do not prime. If you do not wish to antique it, prime before painting. (See *Priming and Painting,* page 38.) Using a brush, paint the body with burgundy. Subtle brushstrokes are desirable for this technique. (See *Brush Painting,* page 40.) Allow to dry. Apply a second coat, if needed.

3 *Painting the top and drawers*

Place the drawer fronts and the cabinet top onto plastic containers or boxes. Paint the back sides of drawer fronts forest green. Paint the underside of the cabinet top navy blue.

Allow to dry and apply a second coat if necessary. When surfaces are completely dry, turn over and repeat.

4 *Antiquing*

Antique the body of the cabinet with a medium-grade sandpaper. Sand off the paint in places wherever natural wear would occur, such as on corners and high areas of trim or detail.

Assemble and antique the drawers. The centers and edges of drawer fronts are also prime wear spots. Attach the top (and the backboard, if not already attached) onto the cabinet and antique the top.

5 *Staining*

Optional: The wood that you have exposed through sanding will eventually turn amber on its own. If you don't want to wait, touch up the raw wood with an amber stain. Dip a rag into the amber stain and rub it into the bare wood. Allow to dry.

6 *Sizing branches*

Get out your dried branches. Position a branch vertically on the front of the cabinet, across the drawers. Mark its length, indicating the angle of the cut. Using a small hand saw, cut the branch slightly longer than the correct length. Cut again to the correct length, making any corrections if necessary. Reseal the ends. Don't throw out the leftover branches.

Position the branch vertically on the drawer fronts. Using chalk or a colored pencil, draw a line centered under the branch.

On the branch, mark the horizontal cut between the drawers. Using the hand saw, cut the branch along the mark. Reseal the ends.

7 *Positioning branches*

Position the branch pieces on the chalk line. On the drawer fronts, mark the sites for screws. Mark at least two screws for each branch. Drill holes at the marks through the drawer fronts. Mark corresponding sites on the branches and check that the branches match up.

Then drill leader-holes (holes that are narrower than the screws) partway through the branches at the marks. Leader-holes will prevent the screws from splitting the branches.

8 *Attaching branches*

To keep the branches' natural curves and to allow them to be gripped like handles, they must be supported about ½ in. (1.25 cm) off the drawer fronts. Using the hand saw, cut several short coinlike pieces from the leftover branches to use as sup-

ports between the drawer fronts and the branches. Assess which thicknesses you need by testing the wood coins under the branches. Drill a hole into the center of each coin. You may need to clamp the coins (or hold them with pliers) while drilling.

From the inside of the drawers, screw wood screws through the drawer fronts, through the wood coins, and into the branch. You may need several different screw lengths, if the branch bows away from the drawer front. The screw should be long enough to penetrate halfway through the branch.

Country-style folk painting makes a decorative addition to richly colored,
rustic treatments. To add a motif to your bedstand, see Country Folk,
page 60, for instructions on a simple, very effective
paint technique using templates.

English Country

A Hand-Painted Trifle Of Berries, Bees And Bric-a-Brac

The drawer pulls came first. Spotted in a California specialty shop, they seemed to mix a sunny west coast sensibility with English country style. The rest of the painting simply fell into place, a decorative, freehand treatment consisting of charming and capricious motifs painted in soft, dusty pastels. Each of the designs is very simple, but in combination they form a wonderful potpourri. If the idea of a dresser in the kitchen or dining room seems incongruous, create a hutch by placing a small, shallow bookcase, painted in the same style, atop the chest.

Read This First

Choose furniture for this treatment that is simple yet chunky. The featured chest of drawers was selected for its overhanging top, rounded corners, flush drawers and funny, rounded feet. The drawer pulls can be hand painted with original designs, although porcelain or brass pulls work equally well. This technique consists of three stages. First the dresser is painted with a base-coat color. If your dresser has a plastic laminate finish, use melamine paint for the base coat. (See Melamine Paint, page 27.) Next, edges and corners are softened with a quick sponge painting. Then borders and designs are painted on each surface. The busy quality of the hand painting is what makes it appear difficult. In reality, it is a collection of simple patterns. If you have a collection of either latex or acrylic paint colors, this is the project for you. Otherwise, start your paint collection with this piece.

BEFORE

A nicely proportioned, solid wooden dresser with an interesting style. The top was scarred and stained – an ideal candidate for renovation.

MATERIALS

- quart (litre) high-adhesion, water-based primer
- quart (litre) eggshell or satin finish latex paint, pale cream
- painting tools: paint brush, small roller, roller tray
- synthetic or natural sponge for sponge painting
- tubes of acrylics (or substitute latex) in several different colors, pale-to-medium dusty tones: blue, brown, gray, olive green, orange, pink, purple, taupe, yellow
- paper towel
- fine-point artist's brush
- easy-release printer's tape, 1 in. (2.5 cm) wide
- chalk or light-colored pencil
- square-tipped artist's brush
- quart (litre) non-yellowing, water-based varnish

1 *Painting*

Refer to *Painting Basics* (page 34). Prepare, prime and paint the dresser with two coats of cream latex paint. Allow to dry.

2 *Sponge painting*

Start sponge painting with a 3 in. (7.5 cm) band of color (your choice) around the perimeter of the top, blending it out into the cream tone as follows. Thin the paint with water to a creamy, liquid consistency or add glaze (See *Glaze,* page 28.) Tear off a chunk of sponge about the size of a tennis ball. Saturate the sponge and squeeze it out.

Using a small pouncing motion, start sponge painting along the edge. As the sponge becomes drier, pat further into the center, fading the paint into the cream tone. If necessary, pick up excess paint with a damp paper towel.

Continue sponge painting the perimeters of flat surfaces and the crossbars between the drawers, using an assortment of colors. Also sponge paint the feet. Wash the sponge thoroughly between colors. Allow to dry.

Sponge paint around the perimeter of each drawer front with a different pale color. Position the drawers in the chest to observe how the various colors work together and whether there are exposed areas that require touch-ups. Remove the drawers. Make any needed touch-ups.

3 *Painting borders*

Now for the hand painting. Paint a border on each drawer front in a darker tone than the sponged paint. To do this, tape inside the perimeter on the face of each drawer with the 1 in. (2.5 cm) wide easy-release painter's tape. Use the tape as a guide for painting the border. Using the

fine-point brush, paint a line close to, but not over, the inside edge of the tape. The line should look hand painted, not like a perfect stripe. Remove the tape.

Add detail to the border by painting a series of three dashes, evenly spaced around the edge, inside the border.

4 *Painting curlicues*

Draw curlicues first in chalk or light-colored pencil. Thin the paint, if necessary, so that it flows from the brush. Using the fine-point artist's brush, paint the curlicue in one movement. Use the chalk line only as a guide. Trying to follow the chalk line exactly will make hesitant, cramped painted line. The lines should look hand painted.

Optional: The tree shown was copied from one of the drawer pulls. It consists of a stack of three quarter-moon shapes with a teardrop shape at the top. Add leaves along the sides of the curlicues by pressing the side of a fine-point artist's brush onto the surface at an angle to the line.

Optional: Add blue waves with dots along the top border and dashes along the bottom border. Paint small curlicues and dots onto the background.

5 *Painting sawtooth*

Tape the bottom line of the sawtooth. Using the square-tipped artist's brush, paint the sawtooth along the tape by holding the brush on an angle and drawing it down over the tape to create triangles. Remove the tape when the paint is dry to the touch, but still soft. Allow the paint to dry.

Optional: The peach in the center was copied from one of the drawer pulls. It consists of an apple shape painted in a soft orange, then highlighted in an orange-

brown shade on the "shoulders." Two green leaves complete the peach.

Add a row of X's along the top border, sprinkle random dots onto the background and paint wavy lines and dots to accent the sawtooth pattern.

6 *Painting checkerboard*

First, establish one line of checks. Tape the bottom line of the first row. Using the square-tipped artist's brush, paint brick-like dashes, spacing them evenly along the line. Remove the tape.

Paint two more lines of bricks above and below the first line, across the open spaces.

Optional: A strawberry was copied from one of the drawer pulls. Paint a strawberry-pink oval and highlight one side in deeper pink. Add seed dots in yellow or green. With quick brushstrokes, add leaves to the top and paint tendrils to each side.

Add basketweave along the top edge of the border, with dashes below it. Create lazy S's with dots along the bottom border and paint random dashes to fill the background.

7 *Painting the top*

Optional: Paint a motif in the corners. Here, trees were copied from one of the drawer pulls. (See step 4, second part.)

Add a second border to the dresser top. Paint dots between the borders and add stylized bumblebees, curlicues and stars to the center. If desired, add an overlapping diamond or lattice pattern in pale cream to the yellow backboard.

8 *Painting the sides*

On the dresser sides, paint corner curlicues and a cascade of dashes, stars and decorative borders with zigzags and triangles in a variety of colors.

9 *Varnishing*

To enrich color and protect the paint, apply one or more coats of non-yellowing, water-based varnish. (See *Varnishing*, page 48.)

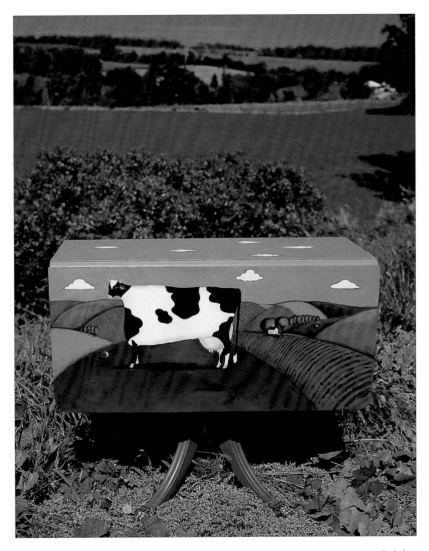

Painting simple motifs, and lots of them, can give a beginning painter a feel for brush painting and the confidence to tackle a more advanced project like the folk painting shown above. (See Creating a Scene, page 112.)

The Cupboard
Was Bare

A 1930s BAKER'S PANTRY IS STRIPPED
TO RICH WOOD AND FINISHED WITH
TRADITIONAL HAND-PAINTED PANELS

This old baker's pantry, with its tin-lined drawers (to discourage mice),
its sliding tray-drawers, and its multiple doors, was buried under heavy layers
of paint and gummy varnish. This piece was worth the effort of stripping to
restore its original slab-style oak and rustic iron hardware. To offset the
plain quality of the piece, hand-painted, crackled motifs were applied
to the door panels and a ceramic-tile top was created
to replace the mismatched, worn original.

Read This First

Just like other easy-to-use finishing products – such as latex paint and water-based varnish – non-toxic, low-odor strippers have been developed and are widely available. These are effective and easy to use. Once the piece is stripped, it can simply be sanded and varnished, or you can paint the traditional, homey design on the door panels. An easy crackle method is applied to the door panels with oil-based varnish and gum Arabic – a clear, viscous liquid normally used by watercolorists as a resist medium and available at art supply stores. (Water-based varnish can be substituted for the gum Arabic, although the results are much coarser and less pleasing. Do a test before applying.) This simple method is more effective than the expensive crackle kits sold in craft and paint stores. The crackle method shown here is subtle. Cracks appearing in the overlaying varnish are highlighted by a rubbed-in brown glaze. (For the type of crackle that looks like the paint is cracked and peeling, see *Crackle*, page 54.) Finally, a new tiled top created for the base adds polish and function.

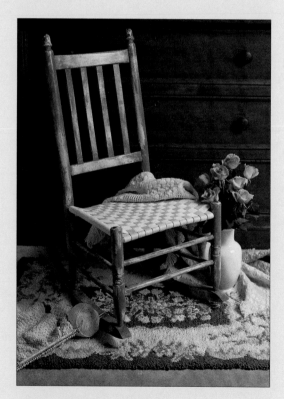

The cabinet featured in this project is stripped to bare wood. However, a piece with many layers of paint can be partially stripped, as was done on this rocker, allowing various colors to glow through and reveal the history of the piece.

BEFORE

A vintage 1930s baker's pantry. Its age, charming proportions and various doors make it a worthwhile candidate for restoration.

MATERIALS

To strip the paint:

- plastic or fabric dropsheet (an old bedsheet is good), newspaper
- low-toxicity, gel paint stripper (Purchase enough for at least two coats.)
- heavy rubber gloves (not latex)
- inexpensive medium-sized paint brush
- wide and narrow paint scrapers
- hard plastic stripping sponge, stripping brush with wire bristles, bucket and water
- cardboard or heavy paper
- oil for hardware
- medium and fine sandpaper (120 and 220 grades), tack cloth
- extra-fine steel wool
- quart (litre) oil-based or water-based varnish
- quart (litre) eggshell finish latex paint for inside cupboard: Swedish blue or other color
- easy-release painter's tape or masking tape, paint brush, small roller, roller tray
- white carpenter's or craft glue, wooden matchsticks
- *optional:* plastic wrap, such as Saran Wrap
- *optional:* brass polish
- *optional:* wood stain

To paint and crackle the door panels:

- easy-release painter's tape or masking tape
- pint (.5 litre) latex paint, sage green (any finish)
- chalk or erasable pencil

- tubes of acrylics: raw sienna, Hooker's green, grass green, emerald, blue-green, olive green, apple green, cadmium red deep, Turner's yellow, cadmium red extra deep, off-white
- fine-point artist's brushes: large and medium width
- pint (.5 litre) oil-based varnish and a jar of gum Arabic (available at art supply stores)
- tube of burnt umber artist's oil paint and a small jar of turpentine, rag
- *optional:* small quantity latex or acrylic paint, cream
- *optional:* small quantity glaze, rag, cloth

To tile a countertop:

- plywood, ½ or ¾ in. (1.25 or 2 cm) thick, good one side (cut to fit cabinet, with overhangs for front and sides)
- primer and paint
- tape measure, pencil
- tile to cover surface of plywood plus at least 10% for breakage. (Small- or medium-sized tiles are more pleasing on a countertop than large tiles.)
- tile cutter (ask about renting from your tile shop)
- coarse sandpaper
- screws to attach countertop to base, screwdriver; or L brackets
- dropsheet
- tile adhesive (ready mixed or dry, mix-it-yourself), notched spreader
- yardstick or other straight edge
- wood trim for edge of countertop (For a substantial look, choose trim somewhat thicker than the plywood-plus-tile top.)
- finishing nails, glue, small hammer (to attach trim)
- paint for trim
- masking tape
- sanded floor grout in a color to coordinate with tile
- tile float
- plastic scouring pads or rags; sponge

STRIPPING PAINT

1 *Applying paint stripper*

Lay down several thicknesses of newspaper or plain paper. Cover the paper with a plastic or fabric dropsheet. On the dropsheet, place the first portion to be stripped. If possible, remove all hardware. If the screws are clogged with paint, remove the hardware later, during the stripping process. Put on rubber gloves. Pour a puddle of stripper onto the top surface.

Use an inexpensive medium-sized paint brush to brush on the stripper. Continue brushing until the full area is covered. Paint all sides, the legs and other small parts with the stripper.

Some strippers melt plastic. Try this test. Paint some stripper onto a piece of plastic wrap. If the stripper eats through the wrap, discard the plastic. If not, apply wrap over areas where the stripper may run off. The wrap will hold the stripper in place and allow it to work more effectively. If the stripper melts plastic, use only glass or ceramic implements, not plastic ones, and certainly do not use latex surgical-type gloves. The stripper may also devour the plastic dropsheet.

2 *Stripping paint*

Allow the stripper to work until the surface paint has bubbled. Check the manufacturer's instructions for a time estimate. It may take half an hour. This first coat of stripper may also begin to lift undercoats of paint.

Using a wide paint scraper, begin to scrape off the paint, discarding it onto an open newspaper or into a disposable container. Let the stripper do the work. Remove only the paint that comes away easily.

Use the stripping sponge to scrub hardware.

Remove any hardware as the paint becomes soft. To dislodge the paint from the groove of a screw, position the head of a screwdriver in the groove, on an angle, and tap the handle.

Place the hardware onto cardboard or paper and paint it with stripper. As the stripper gradually lifts paint from the hardware, scrub it with the stripping sponge and water. If there is still paint on the hardware, apply more stripper. When all paint is removed, dry thoroughly (a blow dryer is good for this). If the hardware is brass (lucky you!) polish it with brass polish. Oil the hardware and wipe off excess oil.

3 *Final stripping*

Apply additional coats of stripper. Allow it to work. Then scrape away loose paint. Don't get carried away with scraping. Too much scraping can damage the wood, especially on detail and trim.

As the natural wood appears, wash the surface with the stripping sponge and lukewarm or cool water. Decide how much paint you want to leave on the piece. Fine furniture should be completely clean of all paint residue, while rustic pieces, especially those that are well worn, are more interesting when they have some flecks of color remaining in corners, nicks and scratches.

When most paint is removed, use the stripping brush to clean the trim and the grain of the wood of all remaining paint. Wash the piece clean of all residue and allow the wood to dry thoroughly.

4 *Varnishing*

Sand the dry wood with medium-grade and then fine-grade sandpaper. Always sand in the direction of the grain. Follow the sanding with extra-fine steel wool, unless the stripper's instructions say not to.

Wipe away all dust with a tack cloth. If desired, stain the raw wood. (See *Staining Wood,* page 46.)

Apply two or three coats of the water-based or oil-based varnish. Sand with fine sandpaper, and between each coat wipe clean with a tack cloth. (See *Varnishing,* page 48.)

5 *Interior painting*

Paint the inside of the cabinet with the Swedish blue paint. Priming is not required. Mask off edges and areas that should not be painted. Use a paint brush and small roller for this job. (See *Priming and Painting,* page 38.) Apply two coats if necessary for full coverage.

Before attaching the hardware, fill screw holes by gluing the wooden ends of matchsticks in the holes. Allow to dry. Then attach the hardware.

PAINTED AND CRACKLED DOOR PANELS

6 *Brush painting the panels*

Decide which door panels will be painted. Mask around the panels and paint them with the sage green latex paint. Allow to dry.

Optional: To soften the effect of the paint, mix some cream-colored paint with a small amount of sage green and some glaze.

Color can be ragged on, or off. To rag on, dip a damp rag in the paint/glaze and squeeze out excess paint. Twist or crumple the rag and roll or pat it over the surface of the panels.

To rag off, brush the paint/glaze onto the panel. Using a rag slightly dampened with water, twist or crumple it and roll it over the wet surface, lifting paint and creating an irregular pattern.

If the texture is too strong, wipe some paint off with a damp cloth to soften the texture.

7 *Painting trees*

If painting several door panels with the same motif or with accent designs in similar tones, paint them all at the same time. Using chalk or a lead pencil, lightly sketch the trees onto the door panels. This will help you to position the images.

Mix raw sienna and Hooker's green acrylic paints (or similar colors) to make an olive-brown tone. Thin the paint so that it flows from a brush. Using a large, fine-tipped brush, paint several long strokes for the trunks and branches of the trees.

Paint any branches on the accent designs.

Paint leaves on the trees. Use several greens for this: grass green, emerald green, blue-green and olive. With more than one color of green on a medium-width fine-point brush, lay the side of the bristles onto the panel and remove the brush. This will give a painted leaf shape. Continue adding leaves to all trees and accent designs, but allow enough room for fruit.

Add apples by painting circles in apple green and highlighting areas in cadmium red deep.

Paint pears by painting pear shapes in apple green and highlight with Turner's yellow.

Create cherries by painting cherry shapes (like a valentine's heart without its point) in cadmium red extra deep. Highlight each cherry with a dot of off-white on its shoulder.

8 *Crackled varnish*

Crackle the surface of the panels. First, mask around the panels. Use masking tape or easy-release tape. Then paint the panels with a coat of oil-based varnish.

Monitor the dryness of the varnish by touching it lightly every half-hour. As soon as the varnish is *dry to the touch and no longer sticky* (this can take two to four hours or more), paint it with a layer of gum Arabic. If the gum Arabic is applied too early, it will form small pools instead of cracks. Too late and it will not crackle. Allow to dry. As the gum Arabic dries, it will form tiny subtle cracks that are difficult to see. Antiquing will show up the cracks.

Note: Water-based varnish can be substituted for the gum Arabic. However, the resulting crackle will be coarse and more uneven. Do a test on scrap wood or cardboard before applying.

9 *Antiquing the crackle*

Mix burnt umber artist's oil paint with turpentine to make a very liquid consistency. Oil paint must be used because the gum Arabic is water soluble.

Brush the paint over the gum Arabic and wipe off all excess paint with a rag.

The paint will remain in the tiny cracks and accent the crackle.

TILED COUNTERTOP

10 *Planning*

Cut plywood to fit the top of the cabinet, allowing for overhangs as required. The plywood can be primed on both sides or on the good side only, as desired. The good side of the plywood, which will be the exposed underside, may be painted a color.

Plan your tile pattern. With the good side of the plywood down, measure the length of the plywood, marking the center point. Draw a line across the width at your mark.

Starting on either side of the center line, with about a ³⁄₁₆ in. (.5 cm) gap between tiles, lay tiles across the front and down one side. If you wish, lay out the full top. You'll be able to determine how many tiles need to be cut, and by how much. The front row will be full tiles. Tiles to be cut will run along the sides and back.

11 *Cutting tile*

If you have rented a tile cutter, do a few test pieces to get the hang of the job. Tile cutters look intimidating, but are actually easy to use. Position a tile in the cutter, flush against the front edge. Draw back the handle, lower it, and score the tile as you push the handle forward. Scoring the tile twice often results in an easier, smoother cut. Lift the handle so that the "wings" attached to it are positioned over the score mark. Now apply pressure to the handle. The tile should snap along the score. Some tiles will, inevitably, break in the wrong places.

Buff the cut edge of the tile on coarse sandpaper to remove any sharp points. Continue cutting the tile until all necessary pieces are cut. Placing the tile in stacks – a stack of back tiles, a stack of side tiles – helps avoid confusion later. You will probably have two tiles that must be cut twice (for the corners where the back meets the sides).

12 *Laying tile*

Attach the plywood to the cabinet either by screwing it on from the top, or with L brackets from underneath. Drape the cabinet in a dropsheet for protection. Mix dry adhesive with water or use ready-mixed adhesive. It should be the consistency of peanut butter.

Apply tile adhesive to the countertop. Plop some onto the countertop, and spread it with a notched spreader. Continue until the top is completely covered with grooved adhesive.

Start at the front. Beginning with a tile on either side of the center line, lay a line of full-sized tiles, flush with the edge and evenly separated. Position cut tiles where needed. Cut tiles should have the cut edge flush with the edge of the plywood. As you lay each tile, give it a small twist to ensure contact with the adhesive. Then lay a second row.

Use a yardstick or other straight edge to even up rows. While the adhesive is still wet, the yardstick can slide the tiles into position. Straighten the tile in both directions. Continue laying tile, until the full surface is covered. Allow the tile adhesive to dry at least 24 hours.

13 *Adding trim*

Cut wood trim to fit the sides and front of the top. The trim should be somewhat deeper than the thickness of the plywood-plus-tile top to provide a substantial appearance. If you have chosen very deep trim, position it and test that doors and drawers clear it when opened. Paint the trim and allow to dry. Glue and nail the trim in place, flush with the top edge of the countertop. Drilling small leader-holes (narrower than the nails) before nailing makes for an easier job, with fewer elephant's feet (hammer hits on wood). For a professional-looking finish, sink nailheads, fill the holes and touch up with paint. Mask the trim for grouting.

14 *Grouting*

Mix the grout according to package directions. The consistency should be like heavy sour cream with sand in it. If directions call for slaking, you must let the grout sit for the time specified. Slaking allows the chemicals in the grout to integrate.

Using a tile float, work the grout into the gaps between the tile. Hold the float with the back edge firmly on the tile and the front lifted slightly. Drag the grout diagonally across the tile, forcing it into the spaces. When all gaps are filled (including spaces between the tile and the edge trim) and the grout is level with the top of the tile, use the float to gather and remove any straggling bits of grout.

Using a *dry* rag or stiff plastic scouring pad, rub the tile to remove as much excess grout as possible. Water is the enemy of grout. Using water to remove excess grout will cause cracks to form in the grout when it dries.

To remove the final film of grout from the tiles, dampen a rag or sponge very slightly and wipe the tiles, avoiding the grout.

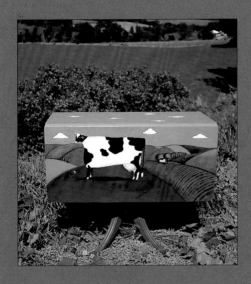

Creating a Scene

FOLK PAINTING CREATES A VERSATILE SEASONAL SCENE ON A DROPLEAF TABLE

Folk painting is a timeless art form, combining naiveté with representations of everyday life. These settings focus on country scenes, domestic activities and depictions of small-town life. Whether stark and simple or full of activity and detail, folk painting portrays an aura of a simpler, cozier time. This table, painted with summer on one leaf and linked by sky to autumn on the other leaf, portrays country seasons with a twist. For the experienced painter, allow us to serve as inspiration for your own creation. For the novice, detailed instructions make painter-perfect results.

Read This First

For this technique, choose basic, plain furniture with simple lines. While a limited amount of ornamental detail can enhance your work, overly refined and fussy pieces will compromise the painting style. Folk painting is an ideal camouflage for a beaten-up finish. The complex pattern and the texture of the paint distract from the damage. The flat nature of folk art, which does not require proficiency in painting perspective, puts it within the grasp of the novice. Indeed, the best folk art is that which is the most unaffected and childlike.

There are two stages to painting a piece of furniture in this style. A basic paint job of primer and latex paint (or spray paint, if preferred) is required. If your table has a plastic laminate finish, use melamine paint for the base coat. (See *Melamine Paint,* page 27.) The folk painting is applied over the base coat of paint. An array of colors is required. This is an ideal project for anyone with a collection of acrylics, or for someone wishing to start a collection.

BEFORE

A nicely proportioned Duncan Phyfe-style dropleaf table. Missing its brass feet, and with its top scarred and battered, it was a great buy at a used furniture store.

MATERIALS

- quart (litre) high-adhesion, water-based primer
- quart (litre) latex paint, eggshell or satin finish, Oxford green (Use acrylic-based spray paint if you prefer.)
- painting tools: paint brush, small roller, roller tray
- access to photocopier
- scissors
- chalk or white colored pencil
- tubes of acrylics: titanium white, burnt umber, mars black, pale pink (or red mixed with white), Payne's gray, pthalo green, burnt sienna, Prussian blue, various greens, browns, yellows and reds
- square-tipped artist's brush, ½ in. (1.25 cm) wide
- fine-point artist's brush for detail
- easy-release painter's tape
- quart (litre) non-yellowing, water-based varnish
- *optional:* paste wax, buffing cloth

1 Painting the base coat

Refer to *Painting Basics* (page 34). Prepare, prime and paint the full table Oxford green. If you prefer, use acrylic-based spray paint. (See *Spray Painting*, page 44.) If your table is wooden and you wish to antique it, don't prime it before painting. (See *Cupboard Love,* page 50.) Reassemble the table when dry.

2 Painting the cow

Place the table on a small but sturdy box or table. The area to be painted should be at eye level; you should be able to walk around the table, reaching it from all sides. (Recruit some help to lift the table.)

Photocopy the cow (page 118) to fit your table. Cut it out. Place it in position, centering it on a leaf of the table, and trace around it with chalk or white colored pencil.

Mix some titanium white acrylic paint with a small amount of burnt umber (to kill the brightness). Using the square-tipped artist's brush, paint the full silhouette of the cow. Allow to dry. Add a second coat if needed.

Draw outlines of Holstein spots onto the cow and paint them in with mars black.

Mix white with black to make a light gray. Paint a soft gray line in the white portions of the cow, near the edge of the silhouette, to make the cow appear three-dimensional. Save some gray. Using the fine brush, outline the eye and ear, and paint the hooves and horns gray.

Using pale pink mixed with a small amount of burnt umber, paint the udder, nose and ear.

3 Painting scenery

Draw the outline of hills, barns, trees and houses in white chalk. Tape the edges of the tabletop using the easy-release tape.

To paint a dark undercoat on the hills, use Payne's gray and begin to paint from the base of each hill up, blending into pthalo green. Thin the pthalo green and paint it as a semitransparent glaze. Paint up to the cow, defining her legs and body. When the paint is dry, redraw any objects that have been covered.

Using a variety of greens (and some browns if desired), paint each hill or field a different tone, painting around houses, trees and other such scenic objects. Use the paint directly from the tube, with very little water; you'll achieve a rich scumbled effect, with hints of the base coat showing through. Lines can be left unpainted along the edge of each hill to create divisions.

Use a square-tipped brush to paint around the cow and tidy up her outline.

4 *Painting details*

Decide the direction from which the sun is shining. Paint the shadowed side of all trees pthalo green. Paint the sunny side a bright green. Paint the shadowed side of a house light gray or beige, and paint the sunny side bright white. Roofs and windows can be black. Add shadows on the ground next to the shady sides of trees and structures, anchoring them to the ground.

Add rows of crops on some of the hillsides. These can simply be lines, dashes or rows of dots that follow the contour of the hills. Use contrasting colors for crops.

Add any other details you wish: lakes, streams with fish, roads, hay wagons, farm animals, fences, tractors, people – whatever captures your imagination.

5 *Painting the horse*

Turn the table around. On the remaining table leaf, photocopy the horse (page 119) and draw the outline of the horse, as you did for the cow. Fill the silhouette of the horse with Payne's gray. Paint over the gray, almost to the edges of the silhouette, with burnt umber, leaving an edge of the gray showing. Add form and highlights with burnt sienna. Draw the background hills.

   Paint the mane, tail and hooves black, and outline the eye in light gray.

Tape the sides of the tabletop. Paint a base coat on the hills, using Payne's gray at the base and blending into burnt umber at the tops. The burnt umber and Payne's gray can be thinned with water and applied as a glaze. Redraw any details that were painted over.

6 *Painting additional details*

Paint the hills, painting around trees, barns and other details, as you did on the cow painting, but use a warm fall palette of yellows, dull greens and browns. Add details as you did for the cow painting, keeping in mind the sunny and shady sides of the objects and the fall tones and colors.

Add more fall details if desired, such as burning leaves, pumpkins, scarecrows, harvest baskets, a church, a mill, a stream, hay bales or wagon rides.

7 *Painting the sky*

Get someone to help remove the table from its perch. Position both table leaves in the up position and draw clouds on the sky. Look at them from both sides, to be sure they don't look upside-down from one side.

Mix white with a small amount of brown and/or pink (to subdue the brightness) and paint the clouds.

Mix half a tube of titanium white and a third of a tube of Prussian blue. Paint the sky blue up to the clouds, allowing the green base coat to show through around the clouds by leaving a small edge unpainted. Drop the leaves of the table, and use blue to paint exposed edges between the table's top and its leaves. Allow to dry.

8 *Varnishing*

Enrich the color and protect the paint job. Position tape in the grooves where the leaves meet the tabletop and place the leaves in the up position. Varnish the tabletop with two coats of non-yellowing, water-based varnish. Allow to dry, and remove the tape from the grooves. Then very lightly sand off any excess varnish. If sanding leaves the varnish cloudy, apply another light coat to the area. (See *Varnishing,* page 48.) Keep the leaves in the down position until the paint and varnish have cured. Then, to help prevent sticking, apply one or two coats of paste wax in the grooves where the leaves meet the tabletop.

Seating

SITTING PRETTY WITH PROFESSIONALLY CRAFTED CUSHIONS AND SEATS

The seat of a chair is more than a place to park. Chair seats and cushions offer a design opportunity to add texture, color and pattern with fabric — along with a higher degree of comfort. Try to find an upholstery supplier that sells upholsterer's-quality high-density foam, batting, and dust-cover cloth. Dust-cover cloth is the non-fraying fabric that goes under the seat to cover raw edges and bare plywood. If you can, take along the plywood base from the old cushion as a pattern, and have the foam pieces cut to fit.

Following are instructions for a basic seat cushion, a piped seat cushion, and a woven webbing seat, along with two treatments for backrest cushions — tailored and shirred. Only the piped cushion requires sewing.

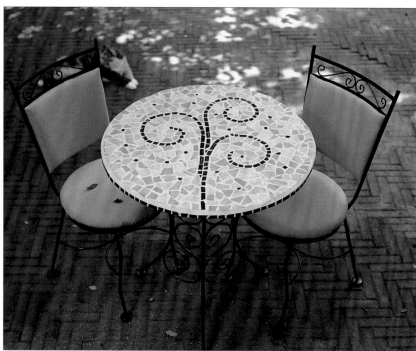

Above, the chair on the left has a basic seat cushion and a shirred backrest cushion. The chair on the right has a piped seat cushion. **Left,** both chairs have basic seat cushions and tailored backrest cushions.

Basic Seat Cushion

Read This First

This seat cushion is the type that looks like a large soft cookie. Use this treatment primarily on round chair seats. Square seats tend to look better with a straight-sided or piped cushion. Choose the thickness of the foam, between one and two inches (2.5 to 5 cm), depending on the style of the chair. If the thicker foam will obscure detailing or be ungainly in height, choose a thinner foam. It will look better, but the trade-off will be a harder chair and slightly less comfort for those sitting on it. Buy plywood that is good one side. This means that one side has a smooth finish, while the other is knotty and rough. The good side of the plywood will be positioned down on the seat. (Good both sides, which is much more expensive, is not necessary.)

MATERIALS

- plywood, ½ in. (1.25 cm) thick, good one side, cut to fit the seat of the chair
- high-density upholstery foam, 1 to 2 in (2.5 to 5 cm) thick, cut to fit plywood
- fabric, 8 in. (20 cm) larger than the plywood both in length and in width
- iron
- ruler and marker
- scissors
- batting, 6 in. (15 cm) larger than the plywood both in length and in width
- stapler and ⅜ in. (1 cm) staples
- non-fraying upholstery dust-cover cloth (enough to cover the plywood)
- screws (to reattach cushion to chair), screwdriver
- *optional:* jigsaw
- *optional:* spray glue; scrap paper or dropsheet
- *optional:* lining (step 5)

1 Getting started

Remove the fabric and foam from the underlying plywood. Clean the plywood as thoroughly as possible, removing any mold and staples.

If the old plywood is beyond salvation, have a new piece cut or cut one yourself with a jigsaw. The new plywood should be ½ in. (1.25 cm) thick, good one side.

Have a piece of high-density upholstery foam cut to match the size and shape of the plywood.

2 Cutting fabric

Iron the fabric.

Lay the foam or the plywood onto the wrong side of the fabric. Measure and mark the fabric 4 in. (10 cm) from the edge of the foam. Do this at regular intervals around the perimeter of the foam. Join the marks to make a continuous solid line.

Cut along the line.

3 Laminating foam to plywood

Optional: Gluing the foam to the plywood can reduce slippage. Lay down some scrap paper or a dropsheet and place the foam onto it. Check the directions on the spray-glue label for making a permanent bond. Spray the foam with glue.

Lay the rough side of the plywood on the gluey foam, centering it.

4 Batting

Lay the plywood/foam onto the batting. Lift the batting up, against the side of the foam, marking the batting at the top edge of the foam. Do this all the around the foam.

Cut the batting along the marked line.

Optional: With the plywood/foam centered on the circle of batting, foam-side-down, spray-glue a section of the overhanging batting. Fold the glued section up onto the foam. Repeat until the batting is glued to the perimeter of the foam.

5 *Stapling*

If the cushion fabric is lightweight, cut a lining from a woven material such as broadcloth. Lay the fabric face-down, with the lining on top.

Position the plywood/foam/batting sandwich, batting-side-down, onto the center of the fabric. Gently but firmly, pull and staple the fabric to the plywood in four places, equal distances apart.

Gently but firmly, pull and staple the fabric to the plywood between each of the four staples, keeping the pressure even.

Gently but firmly, pull and staple the fabric to the plywood between each of the eight staples, keeping the pressure even.

Gently but firmly, pull and staple the fabric to the plywood between the staples. Continue until the fabric is stapled evenly all around.

6 *Finishing*

Cut a circle of dust-cover cloth slightly larger than the circle of staples, but smaller than the bottom of the cushion. Staple it to the bottom of the cushion, starting with four equidistant staples. Then staple between them, as you did to staple the cushion fabric, until the full perimeter is stapled.

Reattach the cushion to the chair by screwing appropriately sized screws into the seat frame and the plywood of the cushion. Work from underneath the seat.

Piped Seat Cushion

Read This First

Making a piped seat cushion takes some planning and sewing ability, although the sewing is actually basic and straightforward. The piping gives the cushion an elegant, crisp finish. Piping is available in braids or wovens, and it comes in a wide range of colors, prints and finishes, from shiny to matte. Choose a piping that will coordinate with the fabric, yet stand out enough to accentuate the tailored edge. If you have never sewn piping with a piping foot on your sewing machine, here's a chance to try it and see how professional the results are. The sewing goes faster and is easier if a piping foot is used. It keeps the piping on track and the sewing uniform. If a piping foot is not available, use a zipper foot.

MATERIALS

- plywood, ½ in. (1.25 cm) thick, good one side, cut to fit the seat of the chair
- high-density upholstery foam, 2 in. (5 cm) thick, cut to match the plywood
- paper, pencil, ruler
- fabric, approx. ½ yd. (.5 m) for each cushion
- scissors
- piping (measure perimeter of cushion and add 6 in. (15 cm))
- dressmaker's pins
- sewing machine with piping foot
- thread to match fabric
- batting, 6 in. (15 cm) larger than the plywood both in length and in width
- stapler and ⅜ in. (1 cm) staples
- non-fraying upholstery dust-cover cloth (enough to cover the plywood)
- screws (to reattach cushion to chair), screwdriver
- *optional:* jigsaw
- *optional:* zipper foot
- *optional:* spray glue; scrap paper or dropsheet

1 *Getting started*

Remove the fabric and foam from the underlying plywood. Clean the plywood as thoroughly as possible, removing any mold and staples.

If the old plywood is beyond repair, have a new piece cut or cut one yourself with a jigsaw. The new plywood should be ½ in. (1.25 cm) thick, good one side.

Have a piece of high-density upholstery foam, 2 in. (5 cm) thick, professionally cut to match the size and shape of the plywood.

2 *Drafting a pattern*

Make a pattern for the top of the cushion cover. Lay the plywood onto paper and trace closely around it. Using a ruler, measure and mark a ½ in. (1.25 cm) seam allowance from the plywood edge all around the perimeter. Then join the marks to create a cutting line.

3 *Cutting fabric*

Cut out the pattern and lay it onto the fabric, centering it carefully onto the fabric's design. If the design printed on the fabric is directional (vines climbing a trellis, for example), it should run from the front of the cushion "up" to the back.

On fabric with a geometric pattern, the placement should match for all cushions. Pin the pattern in place and cut out the fabric for all cushions.

For the sides of the cushion cover, cut strips of fabric, 6 in. (15 cm) wide, across the width of the fabric. Cut the strips to match up with the fabric design of the cushion tops, taking into consideration the width of seam allowances. Usually, one width of fabric will circle one cushion.

4 *Sewing*

Starting at the center-back of the cushion top, pin piping on the right side of the fabric, matching the raw edge of the piping to the cut edge of the fabric. Check that the piping has a ½ in. (1.25 cm) seam allowance. If not, compensate. Pin well. At corners, clip into the seam allowance of the piping, allowing it to bend. At the start and the end, allow 2 in. (5 cm) extra piping, laying the ends across the seam allowance.

Attach the piping foot to the sewing machine. With matching thread, begin at the center-back and sew the piping in place, ½ in. (1.25 cm) from the cut edge.

Lay a cut strip of fabric onto the piped edge of the cushion, with right sides together, matching the pattern along the front edge of the cushion. The ends of the strip should join at the center back. Pin the strip to the cushion top, starting at the center-front and working out, until the strip is pinned to the full perimeter of the cushion top. Clip the seam allowance of the strip at corners, if necessary. If the strip is too short, sew an additional section to the strip.

With the piping foot still in place, sew the strip tightly against the piping. Join the ends of the strip. Turn the cushion cover right-side-out and inspect the seam. Resew any gaps.

5 *Batting*

Using the foam as a guide, cut a piece of batting 3 in. (7.5 cm) larger all around (or measure and cut batting as shown on page 156, step 4). Lay the foam onto the plywood and the batting onto the foam. Notch the corners, so they dovetail when bent down over the sides of foam.

Optional: Gluing the foam to the plywood and the batting to the foam can reduce slippage. (See *Basic Seat Cushion*, steps 3 and 4, page 111.)

If you opt not to glue the plywood and the batting to the foam, lay the foam onto the rough side of the plywood and center the batting over the foam.

Slip the piped cushion top over the batting.

6 *Stapling*

Turn the cushion upside-down. At the center of each side, gently but firmly pull the fabric to the back of the cushion and staple in place.

Continue, adding staples equally to all sides, keeping the tension even. Don't staple one full side before going on to the next. This will cause uneven tension and ripples.

Finish corners by stapling the center of the corner, then folding and stapling the excess down, like a fan, on both sides. Do several small folds to avoid puckering.

7 *Finishing*

Cut a piece of dust-cover cloth to fit the bottom of the cushion. It should cover the staples but be within the edge of the cushion. Staple it in place with one staple centered on each side. Work out from these staples, stapling all around the edge.

Reattach the cushion to the chair by screwing in appropriately sized screws from the bottom of the seat.

Woven Seat

Read This First

This technique is for replacing a worn-out webbing or split-cane seat. The seat must have the necessary dowel-like four rungs: front, back and sides. Purchase webbing at an upholstery supply store or buy wicking for oil lamps. The wicking shown here was bought at a hardware store in a 25 yard (23 m) roll for a surprisingly modest price. The wicking is a flatly woven natural cotton of a pleasing width. But why stop here? Many cast-off items can be used to great effect. Layers of ribbon, bunched yarn, or ends of trims can be used. Torn rags, tied end to end, could give a folksy, rag-rug feeling to a seat. Once started, stick to this project until finished (it only takes a few hours), so you won't lose track of the weaving.

MATERIALS

- approx. 20 yd. (20 m) wicking (the type used for oil lamps) or webbing about 1 in. (2.5 cm) wide (amount required can vary, depending on size of chair seat)
- stiff cardboard, 3 x 6 in. (7.5 x 15 cm)
- ruler and marker
- stir stick or other narrow stick, to fit the width of the seat
- white carpenter's glue and tape, or stapler and ¼ in. (.5 cm) staples
- *optional:* needle and thread for sewing webbing ends

1 *Getting started*

Cut a rectangle of stiff cardboard, about 3 x 6 in. (7.5 x 15 cm). Wrap the webbing around the length of the cardboard from end to end to make a shuttle. Don't cut the webbing.

Mark the center points on the front and back rungs of the seat. The markings will help you keep the weaving straight, especially if the rungs are different lengths.

2 *The first pass*

Stand in front, facing the chair. Begin on the left side. Glue and tape (or staple) the webbing to the left-side rung. (Glue, tape and staples will be hidden by the weaving.)

Slip the shuttle under the back rung, then bring it up and over the back rung and toward the front, keeping the webbing flat.

Bring the shuttle forward, passing over the front rung, then under the chair seat to the back, and over the back rung again.

Keep the webbing even, neat and tight.

Continue until the full seat is covered, ending on top at the front right corner.

3 *Weaving*

Slip the shuttle under the seat to the back right. Bring it up, over the back rung, then under the right-side rung.

Weave the first row by bringing the shuttle over the right rung. Pass it *over the first strip* of webbing and under the second. Continue this over-under motion across the full width.

Using a ruler (or stir stick, as shown here), prop up the alternating strips under which you will pass. When you finish a row, remove the stick and reposition it for the next row. This will make the weaving easier and help you to avoid errors.

Turn the chair upside-down and weave across the back of the seat, as you did for the front.

Turn the chair right-side-up again. Reposition the ruler or stick. Weave the second row by bringing the shuttle up over the right-side rung. Pass the shuttle *under the first strip* and over the second. Then continue across the full width of the seat.

4 *Weaving, continued*

Continue in this manner, alternating the over-under weaving pattern. Stop to check the pattern occasionally. Keep the weaving tight by pushing it together with the tip of the ruler or stick.

About halfway through the weaving, the shuttle may not fit through between the webbing. Take the webbing off the shuttle and pull it through in a loosely gathered bunch.

If the webbing isn't long enough and you need to join it, sew the ends together on the underside of the seat and tuck in any loose ends.

5 *Finishing*

Weave to the last row.

On the underside, weave halfway across the last row. Then cut the webbing and glue (or sew) the end down, tucking away any excess.

Backrest Cushions

Read This First

The decision to have a tailored or a shirred cushion on the seat's backrest is based on the style of the chair. A tailored cushion doesn't stand out. It is an integral part of the design of the chair. A shirred cushion, in contrast, commands attention. It makes a statement, giving the chair a showy, fashion-conscious sensibility. A tailored backrest cushion can be made from any type of fabric. A shirred backrest should be made from lightweight, finely woven fabric. The backrest can be finished decoratively with braid trim on the back side to hide staples, or by carefully gluing the finishing panel in place for a clean, crisp look.

MATERIALS

- plywood, ½ in. (1.25 cm) thick, good one side, to fit chair back (If the backrest is curved, reserve plywood from existing cushion.)
- high-density upholstery foam, 1 in. (2.5 cm) thick, cut to match the shape of the plywood
- fabric (To determine yardage, see step 2.)
- tape measure
- batting, 4 in. (10 cm) larger than the plywood both in length and in width
- stapler and ⅜ in. (1 cm) staples

- *for shirred cushion:* needle and thread
- hot-glue gun
- *for trimmed back:* 2 yd. (2 m) braid trim, 2 small pieces of tape
- dressmaker's pins
- screws (to reattach seat to chair), screwdriver
- small amount of paint to match fabric (for heads of screws)
- utility knife or X-acto knife
- *optional:* spray glue; scrap paper or dropsheet

1 Getting started

For all cushions: Remove the fabric and foam from the underlying plywood. Clean the plywood as thoroughly as possible, removing any mold and staples.

Have a piece of high-density upholstery foam, 1 in. (2.5 cm) thick, cut to match the size and shape of the plywood. Although it is best to have the foam professionally cut, foam this thin can be cut with scissors.

2 Cutting fabric

For tailored cushions: Lay the foam (or the plywood) onto the wrong side of the fabric. If the design printed on the fabric is directional (vines climbing a wall, for example), it should run up, from bottom of backrest to top. Measure and mark a cutting line 3 in. (7.5 cm) from the foam. Do this around the full perimeter. Cut along the line.

For shirred cushions: Measure the deepest section of the plywood backrest. Add 5 in. (12.5 cm). Cut fabric to this depth and to double the width of the backrest. Set the fabric aside.

For all cushions: Cut a piece of fabric 1 in. (2.5 cm) larger on all sides than the foam. This will be used to cover the back of the backrest cushion. If the design printed on the fabric is directional (vines climbing a wall, for example), it should run up, from bottom of backrest to top. Set the fabric aside.

3 Cutting batting, gluing foam

For all cushions: Cut batting 1½ in. (4 cm) larger on all sides than the foam. Notch the corners of the batting so that they dovetail when the batting is folded over the sides of the foam. Set the batting aside.

Optional: Gluing the foam to the plywood can reduce slippage. Lay down some scrap paper or a dropsheet and place the foam onto it. Check the directions on the spray-glue label for making a permanent bond. Spray the foam with glue.

Lay the gluey side of the foam onto the front side of the plywood.

4 Gluing batting

For all cushions. Optional: Lay the plywood and foam, foam-side-down, onto the batting. Using the spray glue, spray a section of the overhanging batting and fold the glued section up onto the side of the foam and plywood. Repeat until the batting is glued to the edges of the foam all the way around.

5 *Shirring*

For shirred cushions: By machine or by hand, sew along the top and bottom edges of the fabric and gather to the width of the seat back, plus 5 in. (12.5 cm).

6 *Stapling*

For tailored cushions: Lay the fabric face-down. Center the plywood/foam/batting section, batting-side-down, onto the wrong side of the fabric. Gently but firmly, pull the fabric onto the plywood and attach with one staple centered on each side.

7 *Stapling, continued*

For tailored cushions: Work around the cushion, adding staples equally on all sides. Keep the pressure even.

For shirred cushions: Don't staple the fabric at the sides yet, only at the top and bottom.

Occasionally turn the cushion to the front side and organize the gathers.

Staple the sides, with the fabric pulled taut. Pulling the fabric too tightly will disturb the gathers.

8 *Corners*

For all cushions: To make a neat corner, cut the point off the corner. Tuck one point into the overlap. Then fold the remaining point under. Staple in place.

9 *Finishing*

For all cushions: Find the fabric set aside for covering the back of the cushion. Fold and press the edges 2 in. (5 cm) to the wrong side.

To make a neat corner, notch the corner nearly to the crease. Fold one edge flat. Then fold the other edge over it, tucking the corner under.

For a flat finish: Heat up the glue gun. *Be careful not to burn your fingers, especially if you are not experienced with a glue gun.* The glue becomes hot enough to cause deep burns, and the glue sticks and keeps burning.

Position the fabric, centered onto the back of the cushion, right-side-up. Pin at the corners. Unpin and lift one corner. With the glue gun at high heat, squeeze a narrow, neat bead just inside the folded edge of the fabric. Lay the corner down, allow the glue to cool and lift the next corner. Repeat until the back is glued on all the way around.

10 *Finishing, continued*

For a trimmed finish: Plug in the glue gun. Lay the fabric centered onto the back of the cushion, right-side-up. Staple the fabric to the back of the cushion, centering one staple on each of the four sides. Staples must be carefully placed at the edge of the fold of the fabric. Otherwise, they will not be covered by the trim. Work out from the positioning staples equally, stapling along the edges of the fabric on all four sides.

Wrap a small piece of tape around the end of the braid to prevent fraying. Carefully apply hot glue to the taped end of the braid, then slip this end under the edge of the fabric between two staples, hiding the tape. Working in sections, apply a bead of hot glue to the underside of the braid and lay the braid glue-side-down, hiding the staples and the folded edge of the fabric.

When the braid is glued on all the way around, cut it with 1 in. (2.5 cm) excess. Tape around the end. Apply glue to the end and tuck it into the gap with the other end, keeping the join as invisible as possible.

11 *Reattaching cushions*

For all cushions: In a color compatible with the fabric, paint the heads of the screws to be used for reattaching the seat.

Position the seat back into the chair. Mark where the screw holes will go.

Using a sharp utility knife or X-acto knife, cut a tiny hole at each of the marks. The cut should break only one or two threads, allowing the screws to pass through the fabric. If these holes are not cut, the fabric will bunch when the screws are screwed in.

Position the seat back in place and screw in the screws.

Joy von Tiedemann

SHEILA McGRAW began her career painting sets and
designing props for major high-fashion retailers. She then moved into the
highly competitive world of freelance illustration, producing art for
newspapers, magazines, advertising and package design. Next she turned to
illustrating children's books. Her first book, Robert Munsch's *Love You Forever*,
became an international bestseller that reached number one on the
New York Times Children's Bestseller List.

An avid home sewer, decorator and painter, she has written numerous craft
books, including *Papier-Mâché for Kids*, a bestseller that won the prestigious
Benjamin Franklin Award. Her books on painted and decorated furniture have
firmly established her as one of the foremost writers in the field.
Sheila McGraw lives on a farm north of Toronto and is
the mother of three grown sons.

BOOKS WRITTEN BY SHEILA McGRAW

Papier-Mâché Today; Papier-Mâché for Kids;
Soft Toys to Sew; Gifts Kids Can Make;
Dolls Kids Can Make; Pussycats Everywhere;
This Old New House; Painting and Decorating Furniture;
Decorating Furniture: Antique and Country Paint Projects; Decorating
Furniture: Découpage, Paint and Fabric Projects; Decorating Furniture: Stencil,
Paint and Block Print Projects; Decorating Furniture: Texture,
Paint, Ornament and Mosaic Projects

BOOKS ILLUSTRATED BY SHEILA McGRAW

Love You Forever, I Promise I'll Find You, Lightning Bug Thunder